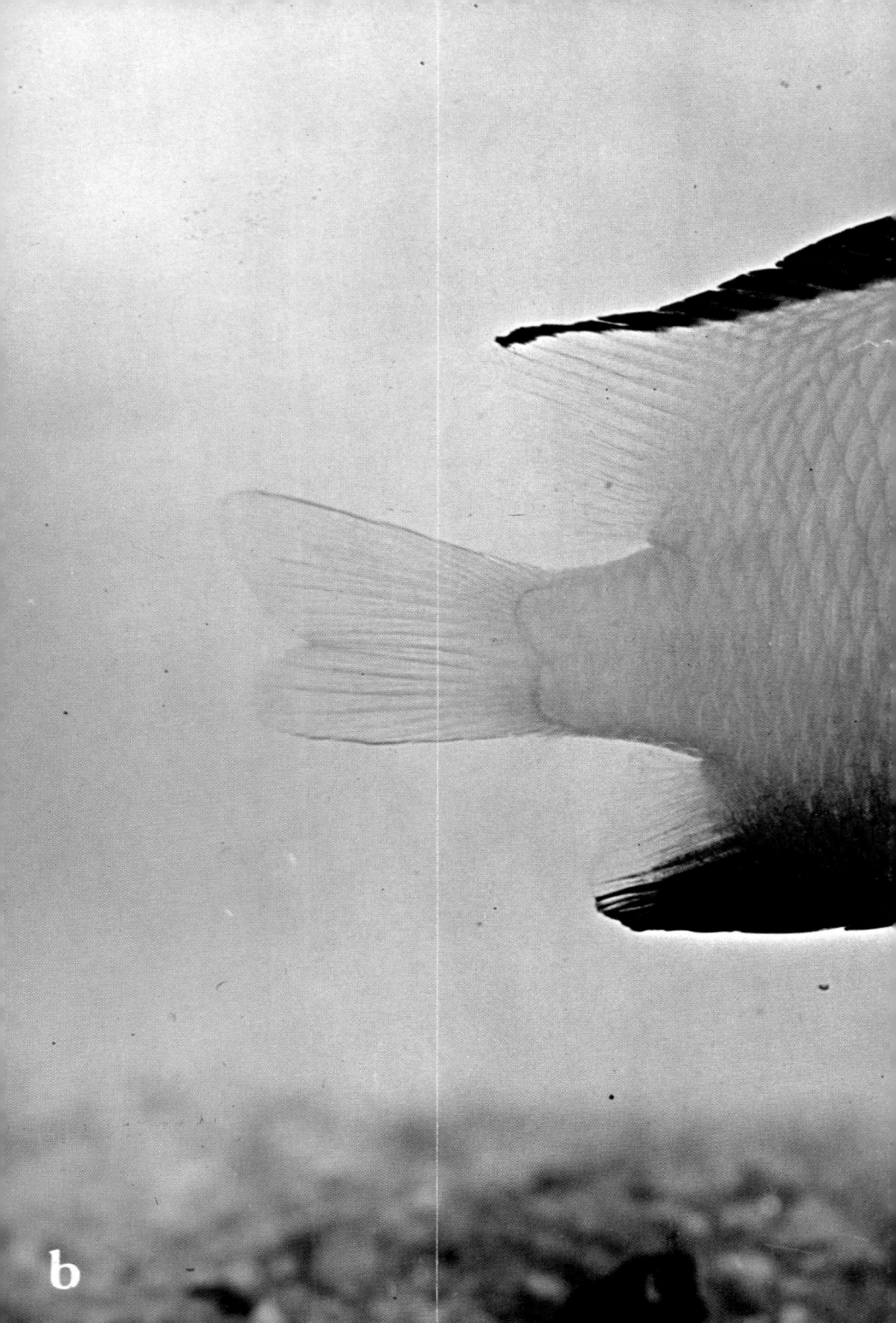

b

Marine Aquariums

William P. Braker
Ed L. Fisher

This book originally appeared as *Marine Tropicals*. It has been updated and enhanced with beautiful color photographs for this edition.

Posters

A = *Chaetodon meyeri*. B = *Dascyllus marginatus*. Photo by Dr. Herbert R. Axelrod. C = *Aeoliscus strigatus*. Photo courtesy of Dr. D. Terver, Nancy Aquarium. D = *Hoplolatilus starcki*. Photo courtesy of Dr. D. Terver, Nancy Aquarium. E = *Amphiprion leucokranos*. Photo by Dr. Gerald R. Allen. F = Various *Chaetodon* species. Photo courtesy of Dr. D. Terver, Nancy Aquarium.

Distributed in the UNITED STATES by T.F.H. Publications, Inc., 211 West Sylvania Avenue, Neptune City, NJ 07753; in CANADA by H & L Pet Supplies Inc., 27 Kingston Crescent, Kitchener, Ontario N2B 2T6; Rolf C. Hagen Ltd., 3225 Sartelon Street, Montreal 382 Quebec; in ENGLAND by T.F.H. Publications Limited, 4 Kier Park, Ascot, Berkshire SL5 7DS; in AUSTRALIA AND THE SOUTH PACIFIC by T.F.H. (Australia) Pty. Ltd., Box 149, Brookvale 2100 N.S.W., Australia; in NEW ZEALAND by Ross Haines & Son, Ltd., 18 Monmouth Street, Grey Lynn, Auckland 2 New Zealand; in SINGAPORE AND MALAYSIA by MPH Distributors (S) Pte., Ltd., 601 Sims Drive, # 03/07/21, Singapore 1438; in the PHILIPPINES by Bio-Research, 5 Lippay Street, San Lorenzo Village, Makati Rizal; in SOUTH AFRICA by Multipet Pty. Ltd., 30 Turners Avenue, Durban 4001. Published by T.F.H. Publications Inc., Ltd. the British Crown Colony of Hong Kong.

Contents

Photography:
Charles Arneson 64 (upper photo); Dr. Herbert R. Axelrod 20 (lower photo), 62 (upper photo); Dr. K. H. Choo 22 (upper photo), 58 (upper photo), 62 (lower photo), 63; Rodney Jonklaas 21; Earl Kennedy 60; Pierre Laboute 19; Aaron Norman 24; Allan Power 18, 57, 61; Dr. Dwayne Reed 64 (lower photo); D. L. Savitt and R. B. Silver 20 (upper photo); Dr. Victor G. Springer 58 (lower photo); Hiroshi Takeuchi, *Midori Shobo* 17; Anthony Teh 59; Dr. D. Terver, Nancy Aquarium 22 (lower photo).

Introduction

After an initial meteoric rise and subsequent crash of the marine fish hobby, marine aquarists have increased in numbers quite steadily over the years due to the increase of knowledge that enables them to successfully maintain marine fishes as well as the availability of new equipment with which to put this knowledge to work. Today transportation is much faster, shipping methods are almost an art, and collecting techniques have been greatly refined. Consequently the home aquarist is receiving a greater variety of fishes than ever before, and they are getting to him in much better shape than they were years ago. In addition, several marine tropicals have been successfully bred and raised in commercial quantities so that in many cases the easier to care for domestic fishes can be obtained.

It was not that long ago that the combination of all-glass aquaria and the disclosure of the effects of biological filtration gave the marine aquarist a fighting chance at keeping his fishes alive for periods as long as those so common in the freshwater fishkeeping hobby.

Although marine fishes are still not quite as easy to keep as most freshwater fishes, one should not be discouraged from setting up a saltwater tank for the gap has narrowed considerably and with only a little extra care you can keep marine fishes without too much difficulty. It is wise, however, to move slowly at first and then as you get more experienced you can expand your horizons to whatever limits you want.

Pearly razorfish, Xyrichthys psittacus.

Keeping a few of the hardier species will give you a good deal of satisfaction and confidence along with the needed experience to move onward. Plunging in with both feet and expending large sums on equipment and delicate fishes will almost always result in failure and disappointment.

This book attempts to point out some of the pitfalls and to suggest those species that are hardy enough to withstand some of the beginner's errors. It also lists some of the more delicate and more expensive species that can be tried once the fancier develops a "salty thumb."

Keeping Salt Water in Shape

Marine, or saltwater, tropical fishes are not generally adapted to basic changes in their environment. To be sure, those that inhabit estuaries and tide pools are subjected to varying conditions of salinity, temperature, and pollution, but it is the colorful fishes that live far out on the coral reefs or in deeper tidal areas that attract our attention. These fishes live in the relatively unchanging ocean that varies in its physical and chemical properties almost indetectably.

For thousands of years many species of freshwater fishes have been subjected to relatively great alterations in the chemical composition of small isolated inland bodies of water and have become tolerant of varying degrees of contamination. Such is not the case with most marine tropicals. It is, therefore, the major job of the aquarist to maintain the salt water used in aquariums in as natural a condition as possible. Fortunately, this can be accomplished to a degree in an isolated aquarium without necessitating the circulation of fresh sea water.

For success, these four primary considerations must be taken into account:

POLLUTION—A condition caused by the addition of a chemical or by the putrefaction of organic material such as a dead fish or uneaten food.

AERATION—Proper gas exchange; that is, the addition of sufficient oxygen and, of equal if not greater importance, the elimination of carbon dioxide.

SALINITY—The quantity of salt relative to a specific amount of water. Sea water averages 35 parts per thousand of salt, or a salt content of 3.5 per cent.

TEMPERATURE—Ideally maintained at 72°-74°F., but can vary safely from 65°-80° for most species.

Avoiding Pollution

Although there is an almost endless number of ways in which the water may become polluted, most can be avoided through the practice of general cleanliness, by having a functional biological filter operating, and by strict attention to the special hazards listed below.

The first indication of pollution, in most cases, will be an increase in the respiratory rate of the fishes. Many gases that form as a result of pollution have an effect similar to that of an excess of carbon dioxide (CO_2), which prevents the transfer of sufficient oxygen (O_2) to the blood and in effect will suffocate fish, even with surplus oxygen in the water. It is therefore wise to note the normal rate of breathing for each individual species so that if an increase occurs steps can be taken immediately to determine the cause.

It is most important that no metal of any kind should come into contact with the salt water. Lead weights used to anchor plastic plants and other decorations generally are safe to use. Water thrown up by the spray from an

Keeping Salt Water in Shape

aerator should be prevented from coming into contact with the light reflector and rim by placing a glass cover over the tank.

When washing out aquarium containers or utensils, be sure to use pure fresh tap water only; never use soap or detergents. Any alkali, such as soap, acts like a direct poison and even a "clean" kitchen pan may contain enough residue to kill overnight.

Tobacco, of course, is lethal in any form, and a room containing a marine aquarium should be well supplied with ashtrays to discourage guests from experimenting with the fishes' like or dislike for ashes.

Paint fumes and insect sprays can do great harm if allowed to contact the water's surface or be sucked in by the air intake of the pump; if a room housing a tank is being painted or sprayed for insects, cover the tank and aerate it heavily, making sure the air is not contaminated.

Corals and marine plants, along with living invertebrate animals, add interest and beauty to your tank, but each will create problems which must be considered. A discussion of coral and its preparation before placement into the tank is presented later.

Many confined invertebrates secrete slime or mucus that insidiously poisons the fishes and often themselves. Examples of note are: octopuses and large nudibranchs (sea slugs), both of which are capable of ejecting a cloud of pigmented poison if irritated. These and certain sea anemones often leave a mucous trail that, upon dissolving in water, gives off a characteristic odor. Many echinoderms such as starfishes and sea urchins also do this.

Uneaten food and other dead organic materials left in the tank are the worst offenders in pollution of the water. Dead snails and other molluscs, along with bread or cereals, none of which is recommended as food, are especially dangerous. Chunks of meat, if left uneaten after a few hours, should be removed and dead material, either plant or animal, should be checked for daily.

The waste material of the fishes does not have to be siphoned from the tank, save for the sake of appearance, more than once every two or three months, especially if your biological filter is working properly. If the tank is not too crowded much of the waste material from the fishes can be broken down by the biological filter. This is essentially a bacterial colony inhabiting the filter media in a filter box or the sand or gravel that covers the undergravel filter. Essentially the bacteria change the harmful ammonia and nitrites that are produced into harmless nitrates that are useful to living plants. A strict monitoring of the nitrates and nitrites of the aquarium is an excellent indicator of the amount of pollution from wastes that is in the aquarium.

The growth of certain species of algae can become quite thick if uncontrolled. When algae die, bacterial decomposition may deplete the dissolved oxygen to the

Keeping Salt Water in Shape

extent that fishes suffer and die.

To avoid algal growth, always keep the tank out of direct sunlight and paint or otherwise cover the side exposed to the brightest light. If growth still forms too rapidly, try placing some well-washed pieces of commercial sponge on the bottom. The algae will tend to collect first on these pieces, which can then be washed off and replaced as necessary.

Some success has been reported in algae control by adding a very dilute copper sulfate or copper citrate solution to the water. Some species of algae are more resistant to copper than others, and if an attempt is made to kill all the algae by increasing the copper dosage certain species of fish and many invertebrates may suffer. The recommendation is to avoid attempting to remove algae by adding chemicals to the aquarium water. Instead, drain off the water and wash the tank and decorations thoroughly.

Occasionally a brown "alga" forms on the inside of the glass of the aquarium and in the filter box, particularly in areas where light reflections concentrate. On close inspection this particular brown film is seen to move slowly as individual specks and appears to be a non-parasitic flatworm, so small that a dozen could lie on the head of a pin without crowding.

Rather incomplete tests run on these creatures indicate that they are not directly harmful to the fishes and probably form food for any nudibranch in the invertebrate tank. They multiply rapidly if ignored, however, and form an unattractive brown film wherever they congregate. Since they probably feed on algae, a method of control would be to restrict the growth of algae.

Pollution sometimes affects to a certain degree a factor known as pH. This is a symbol expressing hydrogen ion concentration in a solution; it is a measure of relative acidity or alkalinity. It is usually determined through the use of chemically treated papers that will present characteristic colors when wetted by the solution. These are compared with a color chart that is graduated from an acid condition of number 1 to an alkaline state of 14. A pH of 7 is considered neutral. Salt water is normally alkaline, having a pH of about 8.3-8.4

Since there is a general tendency for the aquarium water to become acid through the action of decaying organic matter, provisions are made for a natural check on acidity in the tank setup. Pure calcium compounds, such as marine corals, dolomite, shells, and calcareous beach sand, probably act as deterrents to an acid buildup. In this respect it has been recommended that a piece of limestone kept in the aquarium would augment the good done by the natural lime (calcium) corals and sand.

Do not use spun glass as a filter medium. It is difficult to wash out and re-use, as it breaks up in handling, with the result that small splinters become embedded in the hands and fingers. Spun nylon or nylon felt should be used in its place. It appears possible that a good grade of activated carbon or dolomite used in conjunction with nylon may tend

Keeping Salt Water in Shape

to maintain the pH even better, without contributing harmful substances to the tank. Some aquarists use the system of adding a pinch of sodium bicarbonate to the tank each week to combat an acid condition, and another closely related chemical, sodium carbonate, has been recommended as doing the same job even better.

It goes without saying that any buffer system other than the natural corals and sand could lead to an unbalanced pH in the other direction and create an alkaline condition that could just as easily kill the fish as too much acidity. It would be difficult, however, except with strong caustics or a heavy overdose of sodium bicarbonate, to create such a condition.

In a situation in which the water has become too alkaline, a pinch of sodium phosphate or a dash of pure carbonated water would tend to bring the pH back to normal.

For years the big problem in trying to juggle pH was that there were no inexpensive pH testing kits that would work in salt water. Presently, however, suitable pH kits that sell for reasonable prices have been marketed.

The necessity for determining the exact pH and adding chemical buffers to the marine aquarium is doubtful, and one can certainly be successful in most cases without ever having heard of the term. The aquarist who is interested in such matters and wants to check the accuracy of his own kit could carry a sample of his aquarium water to a nearby university, but for the majority of us the system described in this book will be adequate for keeping marine fishes indefinitely.

A last important reminder must be made: be sure to rinse all nets, dip tubes, siphon hoses, and so on with clean water before using, and be particularly sure to rinse your hands of soap.

Filtration—A filter is of great help in keeping water free of suspended material, but it does not alleviate a polluted condition. As a matter of fact it may even help create one. The solid particles of food, fish wastes, and other debris are filtered out by the nylon and dolomite filtering medium where they are broken down by the bacteria of the biological filter. If too much waste material is present, however, the poisonous byproducts cannot be handled by the amount of bacteria present and go back into the tank. Cleaning the filter more often helps the situation (though too thorough a cleaning might destroy the biological filter) but the best remedy is to make periodic partial water changes and to reduce the number of fishes in the tank to a number that the filter can readily handle. Power filters or high capacity air-lift filters are practical for tanks of 25 to 30 gallons or greater capacity.

The effectiveness of the filter will depend on the rate of flow, the surface area of the filter bed, and the particle size of the filtrant. Tests have shown that most of the filtering is accomplished in the top few inches of the filter bed. Consequently, the same amount of filtering medium will be more effective if it is spread out rather than confined to a

Keeping Salt Water in Shape

deep, narrow bed. Sparkling clear water can be obtained and maximum filtering accomplished by first putting in a few inches of broken shell or limestone gravel. This does little more than to help maintain the pH. On top of this should be placed successive layers of fine coral, quartz, flint, or silica sand, activated carbon or charcoal, and finally (on top) spun nylon or nylon felt.

A commercial filtering medium now on the market combines activated carbon and an ion exchange resin. The results obtained using this product are, from all reports, excellent. It keeps the water sparkling clear, maintains proper pH, and is convenient to use in ready-packaged units. It is expensive, however.

When feeding brine shrimp shut off the filter line or the shrimp will be drawn up the intake tube where they will die and decay in the filter.

To avoid algal growth in the filter it is important to cover or darken the entire outside surface of the container.

Keep in mind that the filter is merely an aid in keeping the tank clean. Large pieces of food or dead animals should be removed with a net or dip tube.

Many times a brown alga (a true alga in this case, not the alga-like flatworm previously discussed) develops in improperly kept marine aquaria, coating the sides of the glass and the coral and discoloring the water. An attempt to remove this alga with a filter will only lead to an aggravation of the condition, for it will continue to reproduce in the filter, which affords excellent surface area for luxurious growth. The best solution is to siphon off the discolored water and store it in the dark for a couple of weeks. The tank, coral, and sand should be thoroughly cleaned and enough clean ocean water added to support the fish until the old water has cleared. When the alga has died and settled the water will become reusable. Steps should be taken as suggested in this book to avoid further algae infestation.

Providing Aeration

The proper exchange of gases in the water is, in effect, a way of avoiding pollution; however, it is such an important phase of this problem that it is treated as a separate condition.

A fish, like any other animal, uses oxygen and gives off carbon dioxide. It has been shown that an accumulation of CO_2 in the water reduces the amount of O_2 carried in the blood. Therefore, even with O_2 at the saturation point, an excess of CO_2 may cause suffocation.

Carbon dioxide passes out of water very slowly. Oxygen, on the other hand, goes into solution easily and may be almost at the saturation point even in a crowded tank. It thus becomes clear that artificial aeration is not so much an oxygenating process as it is one that helps remove carbon dioxide from the water. Actually the only thing that aeration accomplishes is to speed up the natural exchange of gases by bringing CO_2-laden water to the surface and circulating newly

Keeping Salt Water in Shape

oxygenated surface water throughout the tank.

Generally speaking, fewer marine fishes than freshwater fishes can be kept in the same volume of water. For one thing, marine fishes are usually larger than the freshwater tropicals kept in home aquariums. With some exceptions, the saltwater species are more active, using more oxygen and giving off metabolic wastes faster than freshwater specimens. In addition, sea water has about 20 per cent less dissolved oxygen than fresh water. At 68 °F., the oxygen saturation point of sea water is 7.12 parts per million as compared to 8.84 p.p.m. for distilled water.

Some species create carbon dioxide at a faster rate than others of equal size. The active marine jewelfish, for example, will generate more carbon dioxide than a cardinalfish. For coral fishes, generally, one or two inches of fish per gallon of water in a typical rectangular aquarium should not cause uncomfortable breathing. The larger figure would apply to fishes such as the gobies, blennies, cardinalfishes, and other slower-moving fishes, and the smaller estimate would apply to active fishes such as the damsels or those with larger gill surfaces, like the boxfishes and angelfishes. A specific example in a 3-gallon unaerated aquarium occupied to its limit would be: a black angel two inches long, two sergeant majors each one-half inch long, and a pair of neon gobies each one inch long.

The safest way to determine whether or not sufficient aeration is afforded is to note the normal breathing rates of the individuals and then place them into the new aquarium. If, after normal excitement is over, the rates of breathing have become obviously faster, the tank is probably overcrowded and some fishes must be removed or aeration employed.

Artificial aeration sometimes permits, unfortunately, the overcrowding of the fish tank. This disaster is usually more directly psychological than physiological in that the fishes are constantly in each other's way, and there will be quarreling in the tank as a result. The possibility of the air pump's becoming shut off due to a power shortage or some mechanical failure, which will result in the loss of the entire group in an overpopulated aquarium, is always present.

Aeration used intelligently is a boon to the maintenance of the health and vitality of the fishes. The worry of the possible failure of the aerator will be over if the tank is populated to just a little above the limit that normally would exist if aeration were not used. If pump failure should occur during your absence, the fishes could live for a considerable length of time.

An air pump that will run at least one strong stream of bubbles in 18 inches of water and that would preferably supply sufficient pressure to operate a second emergency line to an air stone and another to a filter line, which may be desired later on, should be purchased.

Only plastic air lines are used, and an air stone that breaks up the air into fine

Keeping Salt Water in Shape

bubbles makes aeration much more efficient. A system of valves that permits a filter, aerator, or emergency line to be used independently is convenient and usually necessary when using two or more lines at the same time to regulate the air flow.

Proper Salinity

The salt content of ocean water varies slightly depending on depth, temperature, humidity, dilution by rain, and other local conditions. Salinity variation can be detected through the use of a simple hydrometer. This is floated in the water being tested and assumes different levels of submergence depending on the salinity of the solution. This instrument measures directly the specific gravity, or weight of the salt water relative to an equal volume of distilled water, and will generally show a reading of from 1.020 to 1.030 in water suitable for raising marine tropicals.

Salt water in a container such as an aquarium will tend to evaporate at a rate that depends on surface area, temperature, humidity of the air, and whether or not aeration is used. Only the pure water evaporates, leaving the salts behind, so that in order to re-establish the original salinity we have merely to add fresh tap water and check it with our hydrometer. If excessive chlorine or fluorine is present in tap water it is best to aerate the tap water well before adding it to the aquarium. If your tap water is

heavily mineralized, use rain or distilled water instead.

A glass cover over the tank will do much to eliminate excessive evaporation. Salinity adjustments can most easily be accomplished during the periodic water changes.

Maintaining the Temperature

Temperature is usually considered a problem in colder climates only, for a tank shielded from the direct rays of the sun will not often become too warm for the fishes. Aeration with the tank cover removed will do much to cool the water if it is considered necessary, but the rapid evaporation that occurs necessitates a close check on salinity. Temperatures should be kept within extremes of 65 °F and 80 °F, with the ideal about 72 °F. If the temperature should drop during the night below the lower extreme of 65 °F, a tank of over 20 gallons capacity will usually retain sufficient warmth to keep the fish snug until the next morning. In smaller tanks, or when the temperature stays below 65 °F for any length of time, it is necessary to install an aquarium heater. Use the type with elements installed in glass, and avoid the chrome trimmed heaters. Your supplier will be able to provide you with the proper aquarium heater.

Many of the tropicals can stand a gradual temperature drop for a short time to less than 50 °F. They will, however, jam themselves far into coral nooks,

Setting Up the Ideal Tank

barely moving in an effort to stay warm, and can survive only some six to 14 hours at these low temperatures. If not revived shortly thereafter by a gradual warming of the water, most of the fishes will die.

Very often a rapid change in temperature of only 5 to 10 degrees F, such as that which might occur in changing from one container to another, is sufficient to shock and kill a fish. Whenever a transfer is made, the temperatures of the containers should be taken. If found to differ considerably, the transfer should be delayed until water temperatures more nearly coincide, or the temperatures should be equalized by pouring water back and forth from one tank to another.

Hydrometer for measuring salinity of aquarium water.

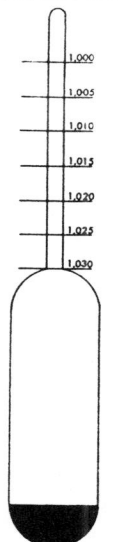

Methods that are used in preparing a tank and adding sand, coral, and water predetermine to a great extent the success of your aquarium.

The tank itself should be of all-glass construction. The ideal size will vary depending on circumstances, but a 30-gallon tank that is aerated usually affords sufficient room for maintaining a nice selection of small tropicals and at least one larger angel or other species of fish some two to three inches long. A number of glass fish tanks that afford a large surface area to volume ratio should be available in emergencies or for experimentation. Although it is a subject for further experiment, setting up a miniature marine aquarium is not encouraged, even in the face of the temptations created by the availability of coral fishes only a quarter of an inch long. The more room these babies have the more natural will be their growth.

Select a continuously shaded area for the tank location and as a further defense against algae formation paint or cover the outside of the glass exposed to the brightest light. Any light that is placed directly on the aquarium should be turned on only when displaying the fishes, except in cases where marine plants are used or when white fluorescent or blue lights are installed, as these do not appear to encourage algae formation.

If an air pump is used it should, if possible, be placed on a separate support above the tank and at least six inches of air line should be exposed above the water. This precaution is observed in the event the pump stops for any reason and prevents water from siphoning back into it and corroding the parts.

Sand

A layer of sand will give a natural appearance to the bottom of the aquarium and afford certain tropicals material for making a home under the coral.

Grains the size of a pinhead are ideal. Most beach sand is calcareous and preferred to glittering siliceous sand, for the calcium apparently helps check the tendency of the water to become acid, a condition due partly to accumulation of the products of metabolism. This check may also be accomplished to some extent by the addition of decorative corals in the tank or by any calcareous substitute such as dolomite.

Regular beach sand or that purchased at a tropical fish store should be washed repeatedly in fresh water until the water runs off sparkling clean. Because some fishes like to burrow in the sand, especially at night, a layer at least one-half to one inch thick should be spread on the bottom. Scavengers such as horseshoe or hermit crabs will continually work through this bottom cover, preventing the accumulation of decaying food.

Coral

One of the advantages of a marine aquarium is that most of the marine tropicals, in contrast to freshwater fishes, have a fondness for the beautiful corals and possess an amazing ability to dodge in and out of the sharp fingers with impunity.

Each tank should be well supplied with suitable cover, for most species make individual homes for themselves and will go night after night to their own selected nook or cranny to rest. If insufficient cover exists and the fishes are forced to find refuge in the same hole there will be quarreling and disastrous battles, and neither fish nor fancier will find peace.

Before placing coral in the tank, even though it be of the pure white store variety, it must be given special attention. If your own collection of live corals is made, soak the pieces in fresh water overnight and than blast as much of the dead protoplasm off as possible with a strong jet of water.

Many types of invertebrates, including shellfish, worms, starfish, etc., make their home in the underside of the coral clumps, so these should be picked out by chipping the softer stem material away. Both the newly collected and any other discolored "store" coral can then be put in a household bleach solution (about a quarter of a pint per gallon of fresh water) for 24 hours. This process also disinfects the coral. Rinse it well for an hour in running fresh water to prevent it from turning yellow because of bleach residue. Finally, and most important, the coral is soaked in either natural or artificial salt water for several days, rinsed thoroughly again, and placed in

Setting Up the Ideal Tank

your aquarium. Coral can be further whitened by dipping it for a short time in dilute hydrochloric or muriatic acid. This process should last only a few seconds or the coral will begin to dissolve. The usual rinsing precautions should follow.

It is best to select corals whose formation provides a minimum thickness in cross-section of any area. This suggests the use of corals such as the branching staghorn, Fiji or buttonhole, or the compressed corals such as the mushroom, rather than the head corals like brain, rose, or beesnest. This is because the thick heads are more difficult to rid of organic impurities, such as burrowing molluscs, and consequently are much more difficult to cure.

Coral and other rockwork will displace an equal volume of water. This must be taken into consideration when figuring the number of fishes for your tank. A 20-gallon tank may contain only 15 gallons of water after displacement by coral and other decorations.

Adding the Sea Water

You have made it possible now, through your sanitation in assembling the tank, to add the sea water and to expect no contamination to take place. The expense and inconvenience incurred in shipping natural sea water any distance and the reliability of the currently available synthetic sea salts have led those who live far from the ocean and many who even live close to areas where ocean water is easily collected to use manufactured sea water in their aquaria. There are a number of different products on the market now that when mixed properly will effectively support marine life. The control the aquarist has over the purity of the water as well as the salinity, pH, etc., seems to outweigh the additional expense of the mix. It is also quite satisfying to the aquarist to know that in an emergency he could easily whip up a new batch of salt water for his fishes rather than having to collect his own from the nearby ocean—especially in the wintertime in northern regions. Be sure to mix the salts as per the instructions as different products are often mixed in different ways to achieve basically the same result.

However, if you do for any reason prefer to collect and use only natural sea water be sure to use from the start only water in top condition, as free of suspended material as possible and unpolluted by sewage, muddy bottoms, or byproducts of plant decay.

So let us assume the reader is located within driving distance of the ocean or intends either to ship in sea water especially or to use the water sent with the fish. In the latter case it is wise to deal with a supplier who understands the problems of saltwater contamination and can deliver the water in perfect condition.

A number of 2-gallon glass jugs with handles for carrying and covers that have been painted with asphaltum varnish are ideal for collecting salt water. Polyethylene bags are also suitable. Water

Setting Up the Ideal Tank

should preferably be obtained from a clean sandy beach during an incoming tide and may even then appear dirty in northern areas, particularly if a surf is running. This condition will be rectified later. In winter or where ocean beaches are not accessible, possibly some fisherman friend will obligingly fill your jugs out at sea.

At home, set the jugs near the aquarium and let the water settle for at least 24 hours. In northern areas, it may take as long as a week or more for the water, undisturbed, to settle, but it usually becomes crystal clear and will leave a layer of sediment on the bottom of the container. For a meticulous aquarist, or if you have unavoidably collected dirty, algae-laden water, it might be well to let the water remain undisturbed for several weeks in total darkness, which will permit any algae and parasites to die. To save time in this case, filtration used in combination with settling is the best answer.

Carefully lift the first jug of settled water, being careful not to disturb the sediment, and place it on a high shelf or on a clean board fitted across the top of the tank. Be sure not to permit water to run on the wood and thence into the tank. The action of salt water on new wood, particularly, creates toxic substances. With a clean plastic hose of large diameter siphon the contents into the tank, avoiding the sediment by leaving some two or three inches of water on the bottom of the jug. The water left in each jug can be poured together and permitted to resettle.

Bring the water level to about one inch below the rim of the tank.

Covering the Tank

To prevent excessive evaporation, keep foreign matter from entering the water in the tank, and to avoid coating the light reflector, filter parts, or other metal with salt spray, a glass cover should be placed over the top of the tank. The ideal cover is cut to a size that is just smaller than the inside diameter of the top of the tank and supported below the level of the top rim by S-shaped plastic brackets. A space for the admittance of air lines, filter tubes, and food is left in the rear, and the air stone is placed so that bubbles rise well forward of this, to prevent spray from escaping.

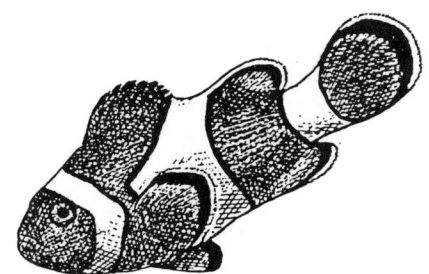

Clown fish, Amphiprion ocellaris.

Cleaning the Tank

Your aquarium now contains all the requirements for supporting a healthy

Setting Up the Ideal Tank

marine community, save for the food, which will not be a problem with adaptable fish.

It is recommended, however, in order to maintain an environment that permits growth and retention of bright colors and to generally vitalize the fish, that at least one-fifth of the total volume of the tank be replaced with new water each month. This means that in a 20-gallon tank, four gallons should be replaced. Any water removed can be settled out and used for hatching out brine shrimp.

Some marine fishes have been kept successfully in water that was not changed for a half year or more at a time, but water changes are still strongly recommended.

In nature the observed growth rate of a blue angelfish, for instance, is approximately one-half inch per month until maturity. In confinement, growth of the young may drop to as low as one-tenth the normal rate, depending on the environment provided. Very often development of color patterns ceases altogether, although body growth continues.

A rock beauty belonging to one of the authors was approximately one inch long when captured, possessed the typical black spot surrounded by the blue circle, and was probably little more than two months old. Seven months later he was a little over two inches long, with the black color pattern spread out only very slightly and the blue circle absent. Were he left in the ocean he would have been some four or five inches long and possess a dark saddle over his entire back, and probably be seeking a mate. An interesting point here is that when a much younger rock beauty was placed into the aquarium, although he was considerably smaller than the first one, his color pattern was more advanced. Immediately he began to chase the older one about the tank, apparently responding to his instincts, which undoubtedly prompt the young angels to chase any younger individuals of the same species—the age being indicated by their color pattern, not their size.

The problem of encouraging normal growth and development, together with factors affecting breeding, is incompletely understood and a source of mystery that offers the marine aquarist an

P. 17: Chaetodon semilarvatus *grazing on a coral reef. P. 18: Clown sweetlips,* Plectorhynchus chaetodonoides. *P. 19: Hawaiian surgeonfish,* Acanthurus dussumieri, with spot bream, Gnathodentex aurolinestrus, *and a soldierfish,* Myripristis *sp. P. 20, upper photo: Brown-and-white butterflyfish,* Hemitaurichthys zoster; *lower photo: Shy butterflyfish,* Hemitaurichthys polylepis. *P. 21: Indian Ocean chevron butterflyfish,* Chaetodon madagascariensis. *P. 22, upper photo: Clown wrasse,* Coris gaimard; *lower photo: Adult blue-girdled angelfish,* Euxiphipops navarchus. *P. 23: Regal angelfish,* Pygoplites diacanthus. *P. 24: Whitepatch anemonefish,* Amphiprion leucokranos.

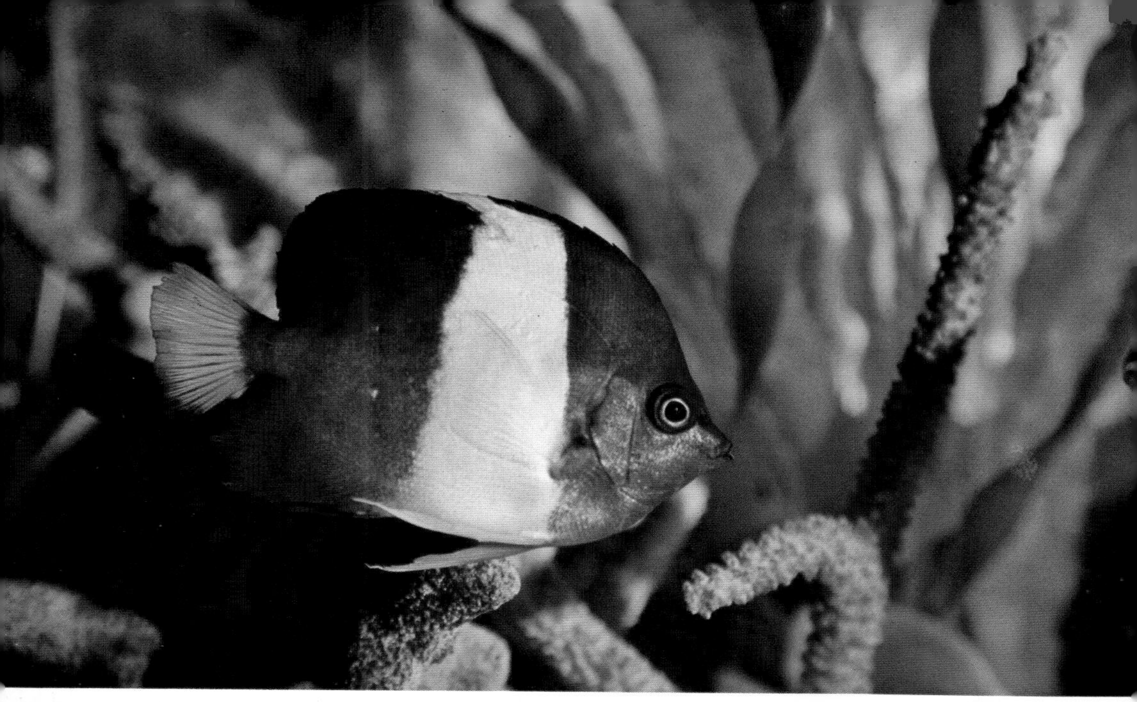

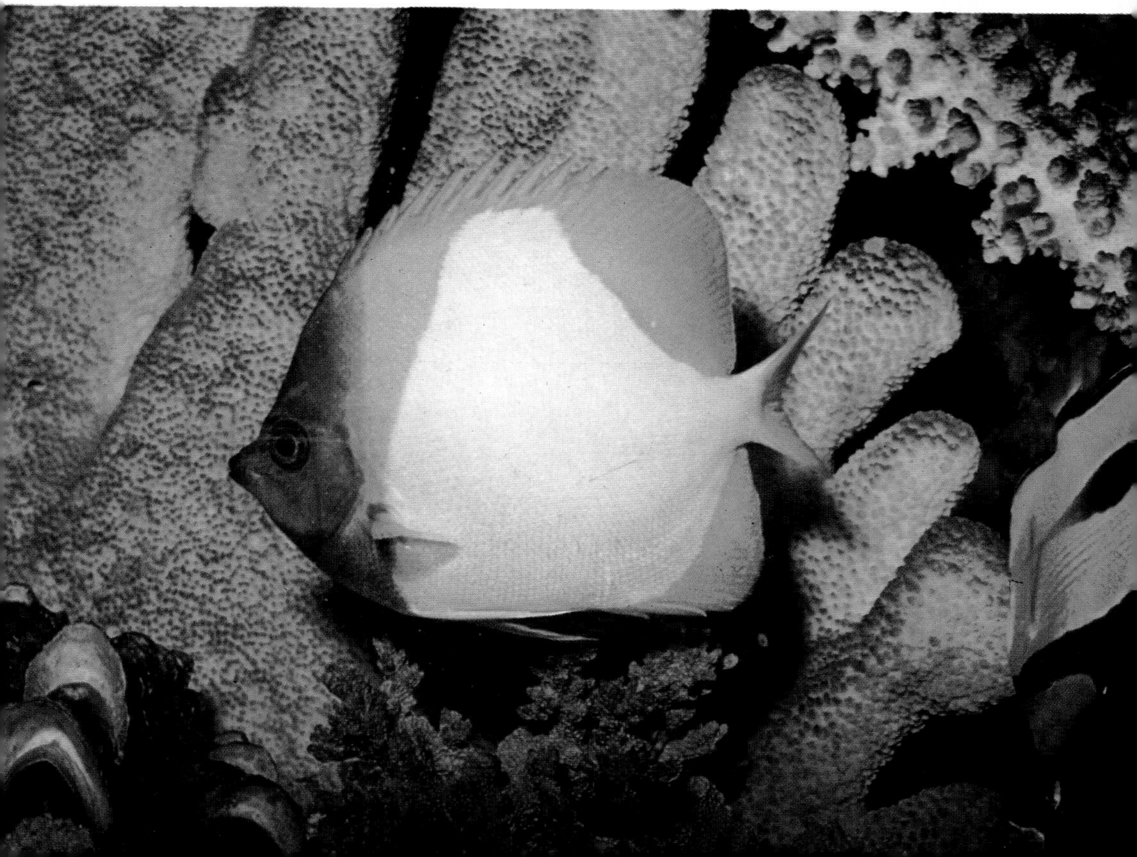

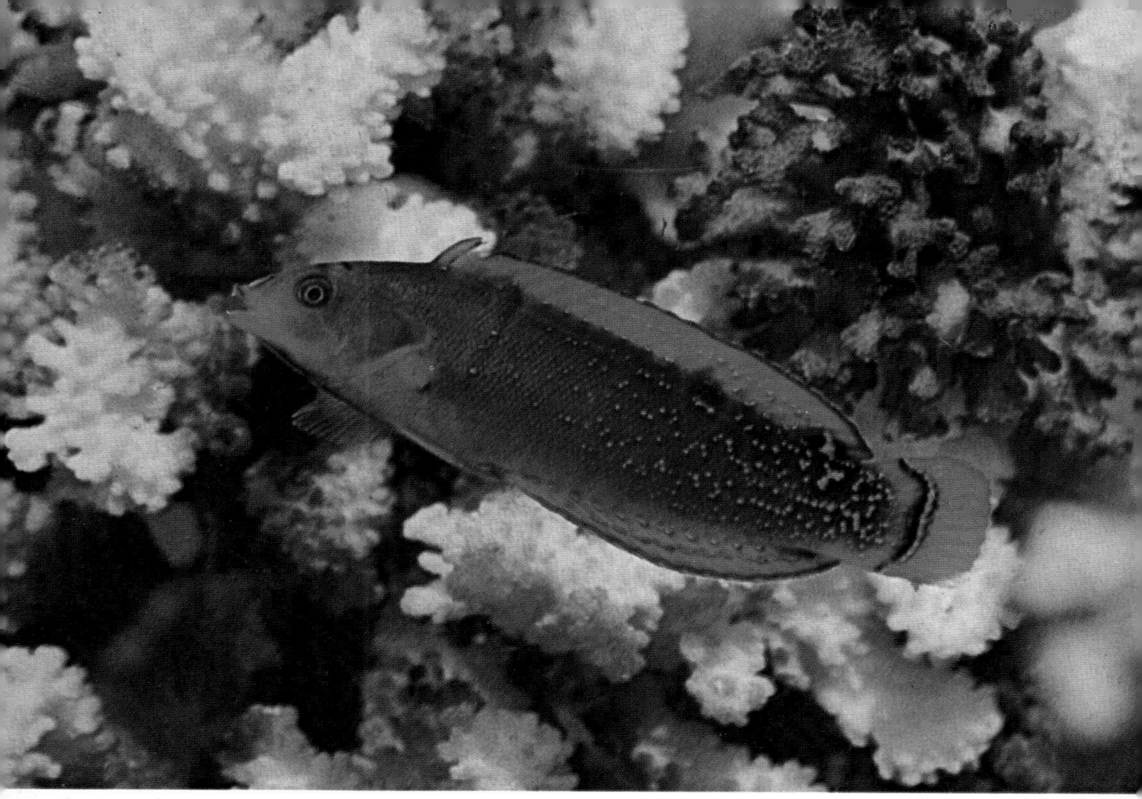
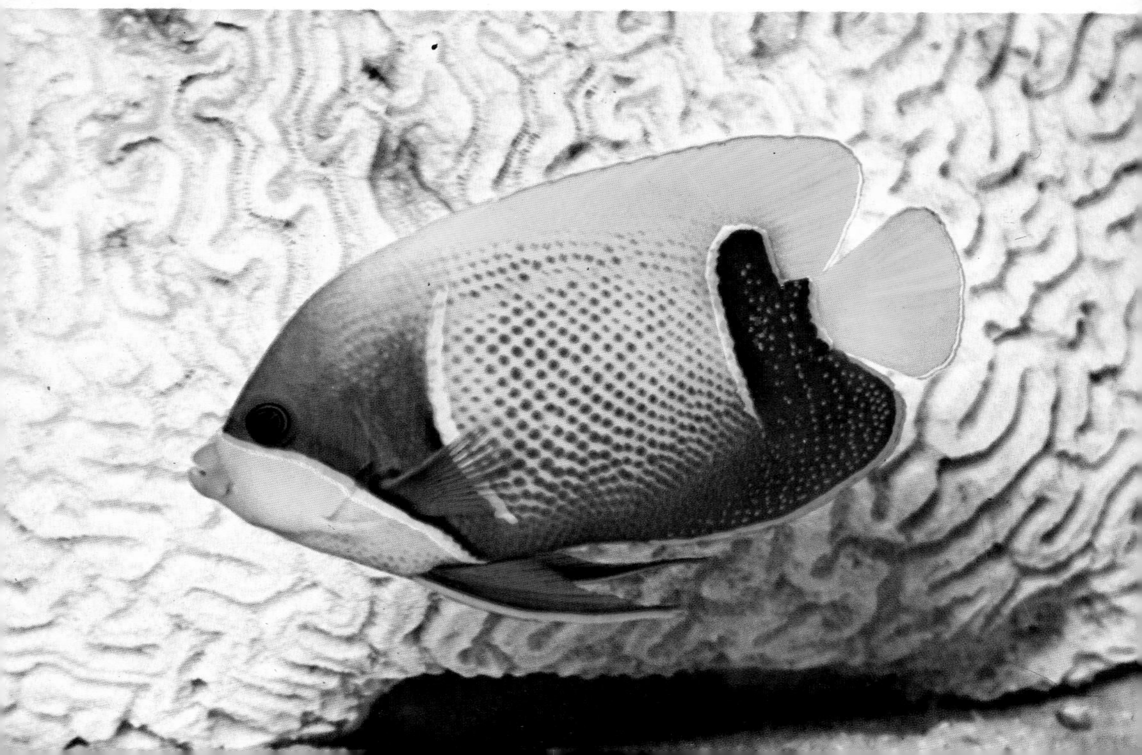

Setting Up the Ideal Tank

everlasting field of study. Chemical and physical changes in the water, absence of a critical food or nesting material, the effect of ultraviolet sunlight, the strong influence of an artificial environment that creates the necessity for extreme adaptation, and an endless list of other considerations all undoubtedly play important roles in establishing the extremely complicated natural environment of the fish.

The time for adding new water presents an opportunity for cleaning the tank generally and giving close inspection to the inhabitants. This can be done quickly and simply every month or so. Disturbing the fishes and the sediment on the bottom as little as possible, siphon all but three or four inches of water from the aquarium into clean jugs. The coral can then be taken out and blasted with a strong jet of water, but if this is not effective in removing any discoloration, soak it in a household bleach solution, rinse, and cure in extra salt water once again before using. After the coral is removed the fishes are placed in temporary containers. Then the salt water remaining in the tank is discarded. With the tank set up on end it can be scrubbed with a clean cloth, flushing continuously with a stream of water from a garden hose, and the sand cleaned in the process. Reset in position, the coral and sand added, it can now be refilled with the old water, plus some new water to bring it to the original level.

Any new additions to the collection are best made at this time when, in the

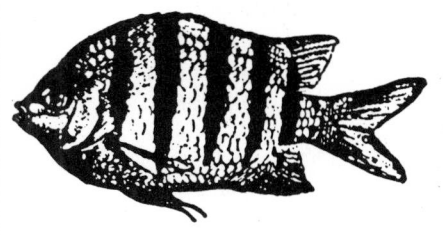

Sergeant major,

general confusion, they will not be noticed as much by the other fishes and resented by the old gang. Timing in introducing new specimens can very often determine whether they will be accepted by the others or torn to pieces.

If a haphazard introduction precipitates violent attacks from one or more members of the tank, remove the unwanted one and wait for the opportune moment when housecleaning.

Corals:
60% water   } solution
40% bleach }
soak overnite, then rinse well in fresh water — Let set in and change 2-3 times

Feeding

All factors in the maintenance of an aquarium interrelate to a degree found nowhere else in nature, and the end result of an unhealthy environment is starvation.

How often have we heard the statement made that a fish "just won't eat" and have found the aquarium filled with polluted water or sickly fishes crowded together.

Many cases of food refusal cannot initially be attributed to the physically sick condition of the fish, but to a poor psychological environment created by the disturbing influence of another fish, noise, such as rapping on the glass or a buzzing air pump set on the tank, unnaturally bright lights, or insufficient cover, and so on. Many times a fish must be taught to come to the surface for food, an unnatural act in most cases, and to learn that the particles up there are edible.

The best possible instruction in this event is the presence of a coral fish that has already learned this eating secret or one of a species, such as a sergeant major, that by nature automatically feeds when first introduced into the tank.

The staple diet for most of the coral fishes should be a good dry food. The fact that such food is inexpensive, readily available, easy to handle and store, and does not need to be siphoned from the tank, should make this a pleasant revelation to the new marine aquarist. Despite all that has been written to the contrary, most of the coral fishes will eat and thrive on this food, particularly if the method of introduction as suggested above is used.

In feeding it is always best to feed a little at definite hours, two or three times a day, rather than to dump in a lot at one time. After a while the fish will nearly go through the glass at the approach of the familiar food can at any time of day, even when their stomachs are obviously near bursting. It is best to ignore this rather frantic reflex. Do not overfeed, and systematize your feeding to save the lives of your fish.

The very young of the angelfish and other species that are caught often less than one-half inch long at certain seasons of the year, find it a long and hazardous journey from the safety of their coral niche up to the surface. Until these youngsters grow a bit and become less fearful of the larger inhabitants, it is best to feed the entire tank brine shrimp daily so that they will be sure to receive sufficient food and have an opportunity to overcome their hesitation to indulge in the new food floating on the surface. Normally they will sample a few stray pieces that fall toward the bottom and soon will be up with the rest at feeding time.

If preparing large broods of shrimp proves inconvenient, keep the babies and other fishes initially dependent on live food in a separate container along with a dry food eater, such as a trained black angelfish, as a teacher.

To keep the entire community in top shape it is advisable to feed bits of raw beef or live brine shrimp several times a week as a variation from the dry food.

Feeding

After a while, even when the tempting live food is introduced, many of the fish will appear to prefer the dry food, but this is probably due to an artificial conditioning.

Some individuals and all members of certain species never seem to respond to dry food, no matter how the subject is broached. The cardinalfish is notoriously an eater of live fishes, as are sargassumfish, snappers, groupers, and others; however, most of these will thrive on bits of raw beef, crayfish, or shrimp. Chopped shellfish and shrimp are recommended for feeding when beef is consistently refused. Raw beef does not decompose as rapidly in the salt water as does the other meat, and it will support the health of the fishes admirably.

All meat should be fresh, rinsed of juices, torn into small bite-size fragments, and the pieces dropped individually into the water. When interest in the meat subsides, feeding should be discontinued and any uneaten pieces immediately removed from the tank with a dip tube. For an occasional treat, live freshwater guppies and fresh- or salt-water minnows can be fed the meat eaters and sometimes, too, the larger angelfish, gobies, wrasses, and sea horses. It is not necessary to acclimate the guppies to salt water. Simply keep them in a separate freshwater container and add to the marine tank as necessary for food.

No food that dissolves in the water, such as bread or cereal or meats other than those suggested, is recommended.

All indications seem to prove that the tropicals appreciate a bit of sea lettuce or other leafy marine algae every so often, but they do not need it to supplement the diet of a good dry food, which also contains plant products and apparently benefits the fish in this respect. It is reported that fresh garden lettuce and canned spinach are relished by marine fishes.

As mentioned earlier, the very young rare coral fishes that are becoming available through scientific collecting techniques and larger individuals of a few other species, although hardy in other respects, are usually dependent at least for a while on live food.

As the marine hobby blossomed the demand for good frozen food designed for marine fishes and invertebrates increased tremendously. To meet this demand many commercially packaged foods such as squid, chopped clams, marine plankton, etc., appeared and helped the marine (and sometimes also the freshwater) aquarist satisfy the needs of his fishes. Many of these products are as close to the natural diet as one can get and are highly recommended.

Brine Shrimp

The marine aquarist was blessed by the discovery, some time ago, of a method of drying and preserving the eggs of a small crustacean named *Artemia,* commonly known as the brine shrimp. These eggs, found by the millions floating on the surface of natural salt lakes and brine

Feeding

Spanish hogfish, Bodianus rufus

beds in which the adults breed, will remain viable for years if carefully packaged.

Here is a system which should eliminate the mystery and unnecessary to-do in aquaristic circles about the successful hatching, rearing, and breeding of these little creatures.

Brine shrimp thrive naturally, it is reported, in water so salty that few other forms of life exist there. They will breed and live readily in regular ocean water, however, so either this or artificial salt water can be used for hatching out the eggs. About eight tablespoonfuls of marine salts dissolved in a gallon of fresh water will afford a suitable hatching medium.

Use an all-glass, 1-gallon fish bowl or jar and fill it with about three inches of salt water. Sprinkle the surface lightly with eggs and allow some 20 to 48 hours for hatching. The temperature is favorable from 70 °F to 90 °F; if much

below 60 °F the hatching time will increase considerably. A better percentage of hatch will be realized if a very strong stream of air is bubbled through the hatching container. For the hobbyist who wants larval shrimp in quantity, there are commercial hatchers available.

When all the eggs have hatched, the shrimp can then be separated from the eggs by simply siphoning the water from below the surface with a soft surgical rubber tube that can be pinched to control the rate of flow. The shrimp can be concentrated by darkening much of the container or placing a light near the other end. The shrimp will accumulate at the light for easy siphoning. Strain the shrimp water into a container through a clean handkerchief or fine muslin cloth. In this manner the shrimp are easily collected and can be shaken into the aquarium and water obtained for the next hatching.

The failure to separate the egg shells from the live shrimp may prove disastrous. This was discovered when the mixture was fed to a number of newly born sea horses. Directly afterward many died, and under the microscope egg shells were revealed lodged in the esophagus of the sea horses—obviously the cause of death.

Before the hatching water is reused, it is wise to aerate it for 10 minutes or so, but it should be discarded after a half dozen broods have been hatched. The time to change the water is usually indicated when the shrimp either fail to

Feeding

hatch in sufficient numbers or, when they do, simply vibrate on the side of the glass rather than swim actively about.

If it is desired to keep the shrimp for a few days after separating them from the eggs, place them into a shallow container with a large surface area or into a regular container that is aerated. The shrimp en masse create large quantities of carbon dioxide, and if crowded into a small unaerated fish aquarium as food they may suffocate the fishes as well as themselves. It is best to feed the shrimp to the fishes soon after hatching, for at this time they are more nutritious than days later when most of the yolk is absorbed.

As a matter of curiosity an eye dropper full of newly hatched brine shrimp may be placed in a separate 2-gallon glass container with a large surface area and the crustaceans raised to maturity and bred. The proportion reaching adulthood, however, does not usually warrant attempting to raise them as larger live food for fish.

Make a paste of oatmeal and water and add approximately one-fourth teaspoonful as food to the rearing container every week. If algae form in the container so much the better, for many types of algae, particularly the brown, will afford added food for the shrimp. Small quantities of dissolved yeast can also be added as food. Maturity is reached in anywhere from two weeks to one and one-half months, and breeding ensues in typical crustacean fashion, the smaller males trailing the female, which is about one-half inch long and has

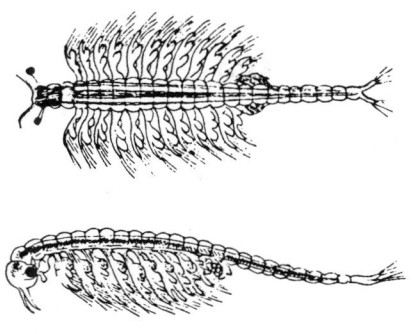

Brine shrimp.

clearly visible egg sacs. In a short while the fertilized eggs float to the surface, where they hatch out in short order just as the store variety with which you started.

Frozen adult brine shrimp have been on the market for quite some time and are available through almost any pet shop. Live adult brine shrimp are also sometimes available in quantity.

Atlantic Marine Tropicals

A discussion of marine aquaria without a presentation of the life that is to be maintained in them is of little practical value. It is impossible, of course, in the scope of this book to mention all the hundreds of interesting fish and invertebrate forms that are available from Florida waters alone.

There is, however, a great deal of general information on groups of fishes and important specific cautions that must be presented to avoid costly mistakes.

Angelfishes and Butterflyfishes

These two groups belong to the families Pomacanthidae and Chaetodontidae respectively. In general, the angelfishes are the larger fishes, growing to one and one-half to two feet, but usually seen at 12 to 14 inches. The largest of the Atlantic butterflyfishes will reach a length of eight inches, but most members of this group are three to four inches long. These two families can be positively separated by the presence of preopercular (situated in front of the gill cover) spines in the angelfishes; the butterflyfishes do not possess these spines.

Angelfishes

The most beautiful fishes on the reefs are without question the angelfishes. The young are particularly vivid, their colors and patterns changing systematically with growth to the more subdued beauty of the adult. Angelfishes are charactistically hardy in the home aquarium. Even when less than an inch long, they take to dry food readily; if selected with attention to size and species, they are compatible with members of their own and other families. The species found in Florida are the gray, French, blue, and queen angelfishes and the rock beauty. The "Townsend" angelfish, long thought to be a separate species, is just a hybrid of the blue and queen angelfishes.

In considering which of the immature tropicals to select for your aquarium we can disregard the question of sex, as dissection would be the only method of determining the answer.

The situations that arise when placing fishes together, particularly the angelfishes, are so extreme that it is difficult to advise on many combinations. From experience, however, we will hazard the following recommendation for a peaceful or at least harmless relationship in a community tank— angelfish of the same species should differ in size by at least one inch (the greater the difference the more peaceful the relationship). For instance: three gray angels (*Pomacanthus arcuatus*) in the same tank might run in sizes of one-half inch, one and one-half inches, and three inches. Usually if two gray angels of nearly equal size are placed together a fight to the death ensues. In mixing different species of angels it is usually wise to keep the French or gray just a little larger than the queen; in any collection of angels the blue should be the smallest of all, since it represents the most aggressive species. It is more difficult to introduce a new fish into an established tank than to start a successful group of all new fishes. This is particularly true when considering the angelfishes. In many cases in which there is an established angel in an aquarium and an attempt is made to introduce another larger one of the same or another species, the smaller one, particularly a blue, will run the stranger ragged, evidently feeling his home has been invaded. If the two had been introduced simultaneously, the larger one would invariably have the upper hand. Where a smaller fish is aggressive toward a larger one of the same species, real damage is seldom done, and the provoker will almost always quiet down and accept the newcomer. Should it be the larger one who is aggressive, the fish should be separated before serious injury occurs.

Angelfishes inflict serious wounds by using a prominent spine at the base of the preopercle, or false gill plate, as a rapier, and in a flurry of slashes can put an adversary away in the first encounter. Even the tiny angels, less than one-half inch long, will engage each other in fatal battle.

Very young rock beauties less than one inch long, as distinct from the other angels, will at times actually be friendly toward members of their own kind of the same age, often sharing the same hole together in the coral. Older individuals, however, like any of the other angels, will tend to discriminate against the younger ones and will rule the tank if their size permits.

Distinction between immature gray and French angels can be made by noting the trailing edge of the tailfin, which in the gray is straight and transparent and in the French is convex and has a yellow border. With growth the yellow bands are lost entirely in the adult gray angel. A partial yellow band *may* be present in young adult French angels, and each scale is edged in yellow.

Separation between the young queen and the blue is usually difficult unless both are available for comparison. When less than an inch long the color patterns are identical, but the queen is orange in areas where the blue angel is yellow. With further growth an orange streak appears on the dorsal and anal fins of the queen, and the white bars on both species first multiply and then disappear in the adult. The mature queen possesses a dark blue ocellus on the forehead, and the pectoral and tail fins are entirely orange-yellow, while on the fins of the blue there is only a yellow band.

A young rock beauty when but an inch or so long is solid orange with a large black ocellus on the back, bordered by a brilliant blue circle. The rims of the eyes also have this same bright blue, and they retain this coloration in the adult stage. As growth continues the black spot spreads to a rich jet black saddle across the back, the blue circle becoming first a crescent and then disappearing, and the borders of the anal and dorsal fins become blushed with red and edged with

Atlantic Marine Tropicals

black, making this the most strikingly beautiful fish on the reef.

One of the more infrequent fish to turn up in collections, but also one of the prettiest, is the pygmy angelfish, or cherubfish. The color of the body is a deep blue to purple and that of the head a bright orange-yellow. This little fellow grows up three to four inches in length and is a fairly hardy aquarium fish. It feeds well on live brine shrimp but will accept other foods such as beef, shrimp, and scallops. It is also a constant nibbler on algae, so an occasional bit of spinach or kale with the regular food would do no harm.

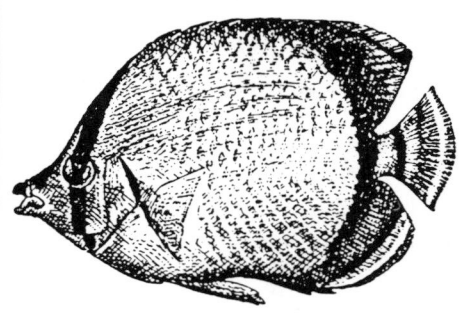

Chaetodon ocellatus.

Butterflyfishes

In a brilliantly colored aquarium of angelfishes, damselfishes, wrasses, and gobies, the quiet beauty of butterflyfishes is outstanding. Their shiny white and delicate yellows, blushed with pale orange, provide an endless combination of colors. This is punctuated in some cases by a prominent dark spot and in others by broad, bold bars.

The foureye, spotfin or common, banded longsnout, and reef butterflies are found in Florida waters. The banded, however, is much more common in the Bahamas, 50 miles to the east. All of these except the longsnout have a black band running from the top of the head through the eye and down onto the cheek. Both the foureye and spotfin have a posterior eyespot. That of the foureye is very dark, with a white ring, and is located on the body, whereas that of the spotfin is non-ocellated, pale, and at the base of the soft dorsal. The reef butterfly may be confused with the spotfin, except that it has a vertical black band along the posterior edge of the dorsal fin, extending down across the caudal peduncle and edge of the anal fin.

When very young these fishes tend to resent others of the same species and age, but with ample space they may be kept in a common aquarium. The butterflyfishes defend themselves by lowering the head and butting an adversary with the erected dorsal spines, but they rarely inflict serious wound. The adults are found in small schools or in pairs on the outer reefs, and in an aquarium a congenial pair is constantly together, presenting an altogether homey appearance. Of the above species, the reef butterfly is the hardiest and best eater in captivity.

Atlantic Marine Tropicals

The young are likely to be dependent on live brine shrimp, as are some adults, for an indefinite period, but many soon learn to eat either flake food or strips of fresh beef. Because of this reluctance to eat in captivity the butteflyfishes are generally difficult to keep for more than a few months in a standing community tank. In nature they are often observed feeding on corals or picking parasites from the larger fishes, which suggests that perhaps these organisms may be necessary items in their diet.

Damselfishes
For aquaria, the smaller size damsels (family Pomacentridae) are desirable. The larger specimens not only lack the brilliant iridescence of the very young but also are aggressive toward members of their own and other species. These fishes show strong territoriality and for this reason should be given a lot of room and plenty of hiding places. Fortunately, the most attractive species are available in tiny sizes at varying seasons of the year, and their hardiness at an early age suggests no reason for their absence in the marine tank. If confined to sizes under one inch in length, several different species may be kept in a community tank, and darting hither and thither through the coral they afford a pleasant vitality to the aquarium.

The beau gregory is one of the most available of the damsels. It is divided horizontally by color with bright blue on the head and back and yellow on the stomach and tail. Little yellow belly, as he is sometimes called, is sprinkled with small iridescent blue spots on his nose and punctuated with a large ocellus of the same color on the back. These pretty little fish are quite often found in empty conch shells.

Sergeant majors or—as they are sometimes called—cockeye pilots or prison fish are the quaint little yellow and black vertically striped fish found in numbers about the wharves and jetties of tropical Caribbean waters. In the aquarium they bustle energetically above and around the coral, and a number of small individuals, unlike most of the other damsels, will characteristically school togther. This hardy little fish will be the first new member of the tank up for dry food, and he gets along with everything in the tank provided he is introduced at well under an inch in length. In a tank that contains slow-eating live food dependent species, the sergeant major should be excluded, for he is an extremely rapid eater and often cleans up the brine shrimp before the others have taken but a few mouthfuls.

Of the other damsel species, the threespot or orange damselfish is noteworthy for its ability to keep the rich orange color of its entire body. This color is broken only by the dark eyes and the threespots that are found at the base of the pectoral fin, on the dorsal fin, and on the caudal peduncle. The dusky or scarletback damselfish can be recognized by the reddish orange streak along the base of the dorsal fin and the light edged dorsal spot. The cocoa damselfish is brownish, with a dorsal spot. These three pomacentrids become a nondescript blackish-brown at about two and one-half to three inches and are difficult to separate at this stage. The bicolor damsel, however, retains its distinctive pattern. It is a handsome species having the anterior two-thirds of the body dark and the rest of the body and tail abruptly light.

Very few animals can compare in beauty with the young yellowtail damselfish, or marine jewelfish, whose gorgeous, glowing color is accentuated with a sparkling personality. The deep blue body is entirely sprinkled with iridescent stars, like a midnight sky, and the fins are bordered by a powder blue ridge.

No marine tropical enjoys artificial aeration more than does this fiery little fish, who will express his appreciation and reward the aquarist with a radiant display of blue. If things are uncomfortable, however, you won't recognize the dull brown little introvert in the corner of your tank.

In this species the young, under three inches long, will have a transparent tail, but with continuing growth this becomes pigmented with bright yellow, and the stars on his body, save on the head area, disappear. One of the largest fishes of this family, it sometimes measures nearly a foot in length, but this size is unusual. Its normal adult size is seven to eight inches.

Exhibiting none of the typical habits of the other damsels is a lovely little inhabitant of the Gulf Stream named simply the reef fish, or more correctly the blue chromis. With its swallow tail and graceful iridescent blue streamlined body, it reminds one of some exotic bird perched in mid-air as it hovers above the coral. Together with a beautiful pink wrasse and other small fishes, young blue chromis are usually found swimming in small schools; in an aquarium they will swim together and do fairly well, provided they are initially fed brine shrimp and the water is kept well aerated.

Wrasses

Even in tiny sizes under one-half inch in length, the young purple and yellow Spanish hogfish displays the characteristic of swimming in attendance on the larger fishes in the tank. All delight in the attention of this gentle little nibbler, particularly the angels, who will back up slowly, turn on their sides, and offer themselves for inspection when it approaches.

Along with other interesting features, the wrasses possess an amazing assortment of resting positions, depending on the species. One of the most bizarre is that of the young bluehead, who in the evening lies down on his side in a shallow depression in the sand and spreads a transparent bubble from a secretion that is exuded from his body to completely cover himself. If the bubble is touched the bluehead is

Atlantic Marine Tropicals

immediately alarmed and scurries to safety. Others are not as neat in their habits. When feeling sleepy or when alarmed, they merely dive head first into the sand, and if it is deep enough they will completely submerge.

The pearly razorfish is a beautiful pearly-white fish usually found hovering over the hole that it constructs as a nest in the sand bottom. It seldom strays far from this retreat, feeding on organisms that float by with the currents. If frightened it will deftly slide down into the hole tail first. Because of its knife-edged head and extremely thin body it can move easily under the sand. In the aquarium the hardy young feed on brine shrimp and other live foods and may learn to eat dry food, ground fresh shrimp, and lean beef. The normal adult size is about seven inches.

Probably the most common of the Florida and Bahama wrasses is the slippery dick. Fish of this species are present almost everywhere and appear like a horde of locusts whenever a baited trap is set for larger fishes. These fish are highly variable in color and pattern. Most are small, about five inches, but some reach a foot in length.

Groupers

Some of the marine realm's richest and most brilliant colors are displayed by a grouper called the royal gramma. Once this fish was thought to be very rare and live only in deep water. It is a rather common fish, however, living upside-down under ledges and in holes, in both deep and shallow water. It displays an inexpressibly bright purple-red and orange brilliance, while most other fishes in its family exhibit camouflage patterns and dull coloration when viewed in their natural habitat. Like others in its family, the royal gramma appreciates a live minnow or guppy at mealtime, but it will thrive on a diet of raw beef and frozen and flake foods.

Gobies

Another welcome member of the back-scratching variety is the neon goby. Several broad bright neon blue and black bands extend the entire length of this interesting discovery, save for a pink area around the gills. If selected carefully, no other saltwater species so intimately pairs itself as does this. They will swim and feed together, cooperate in making a common nest under a piece of coral by shoveling sand out with their fins, and generally give the impression of wanting to be Mr. and Mrs. Goby. If another neon goby is introduced it will promptly be run ragged by one or both of the pair, unless it is a particularly tiny one, and if so several may be introduced without danger. Many in a tank get along all right together. A compatible pair of gobies must be selected with careful observation of a group, for if they are placed in a tank haphazardly, continual quarreling will result. The neon goby has the ventral fins fused to form a sucking disc that enables it to rest on the side of the glass or upside down on the coral, hop on the backs of the larger fishes to search for objects of interest, and otherwise perform amazing gymnastics. The tiny young require brine shrimp at first, but after growing to about three-fourths of an inch will take dry food as well as the larger ones, and they will become the most compatible and hardiest members of a well-kept aquarium.

Neon gobies have spawned in marine aquariums on a number of occasions and the young have been raised successfully.

Cardinalfishes

The cardinal adds a bit of red to the marine tank. It is a nocturnal species but soon learns to come out from hiding and will join the watery society as a peaceful citizen of the group, except for its habit of gulping down small bite-size fishes that happen by. Although this fish has a large mouth, young angels, damsels, and gobies are not normally included in his diet, and if it is introduced while still small it will be quite satisfied with a piece of raw beef every day with an occasional guppy thrown in. This fish should be provided with a conch shell in which to hide.

Blennies

Blennies form a diverse and large family of interesting, queer-looking fishes that are characterized by a single long dorsal fin, elongated body, and—in some cases—stumpy leg-like fins with which they scuttle about the coral and sand. Rooting in this manner, they act as excellent scavengers.

The blennies are common in shallow water in tidepools and over coral reefs and rocky bottoms. They frequently can be seen perched on a rock and propped up on their ventral fins as if surveying their little world. Any movement sends them scurrying for their holes, from which they soon reappear.

One of the most pert-looking members of this family is the Molly Miller, which is recognized by the red fringe on its head. Another Florida species is the bluethroat pikeblenny, a tube-dwelling form that vigorously maintains its territory. Bluethroat pikeblennies make themselves look fierce by erecting their long dorsal fins, opening their mouths, and flaring their gill covers.

Cubbyu, Jackknife-Fish, and Spotted Drum

From the family of croakers comes one of the most intriguing shapes to be found among the coral fishes. Possessed of conspicuously extended dorsal and ventral fins and ribbon-like tail, tiny cubbyus look like little mayflies dancing above the sea urchins that offer protecting spines to hide under should danger approach. The pattern of seven dark horizontal stripes on a light background is not fully evident in juvenile specimens. With age the stripes become more distinct, and it appears that they are increasing in number. In addition, the length of the fins becomes actually and relatively shorter. Full-grown cubbyus are usually no larger than 10 inches and retain the long ribbon-like tail.

A similar form, which is easily confused with the cubbyu, is the striped drum. This species can be easily recognized, however, by the three triangularly placed spots on the nose.

The jackknife-fish is a handsome species, generally larger than the cubbyu. It is marked by three prominent black stripes. The first is vertical and passes through the eye, the second is oblique and extends from the forehead down to and onto the pelvic fins, and the third gently slopes from the base of the black knife-like dorsal fin to and onto the caudal fin.

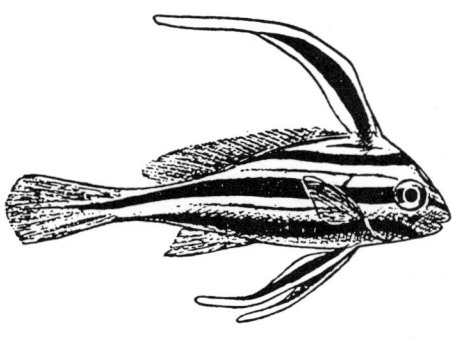

Cubbyu, Eques acuminatus.

The spotted drum is a rare form, found in deeper water than the other species. Anteriorly it is marked with vertical bands. Behind the head it displays horizontal stripes. In addition, the dorsal, anal, and caudal fins are covered with small white dots.

The cubbyu and striped drum are eager eaters, taking almost anything offered them. Ground fresh shrimp and brine shrimp are satisfactory. The jackknife and spotted drum, however, are more difficult to keep and do not accept food as readily. They seem to be fond of the insect larvae known as bloodworms (*Chironomus*) and perhaps should be started on this food until acclimated.

The young are difficult to keep in a community tank, for they are characteristically shy and normally refuse all food except live brine shrimp. Some will learn to take small strips of beef, however, and at least one exceptional individual only about one and one-half inches long has been known to compete aggressively with damsels and angelfishes for flake food floating on the surface.

Jawfishes

The jawfishes are an exceptionally interesting group. They are burrowing fishes that excavate their holes by scooping up and carrying out mouthful after mouthful of sand and pebbles. These holes may be 18 inches deep and lined with carefully fitted stones to keep them from collapsing.

They guard their areas very carefully, standing on their tails over the entrance to their burrows. If another jawfish approaches too closely he is met by the occupant, who threatens it with open mouth, flared opercles, and erected dorsal fin. Usually this is sufficient to drive off the intruder, but sometimes there is considerable dancing around, each antagonist daring the other to land the first blow. If a larger fish appears suddenly on the scene they turn tail and flash head first down the hole, but if an intruder approaches slowly and cautiously all of the jawfishes will slide slowly tail first into their retreats.

Any specimen kept in an aquarium should be given fairly deep sand, a rock to burrow under, and pea gravel with which to line the entrance to its hole. Either live or frozen adult brine shrimp is good table fare for this fish.

Grass and Sargassum Fishes

Aside from the endless list of young fishes found on the ocean reefs, there is an almost equally enormous number of species that inhabit the grass flats and floating sargassum weeds. Most are bizarre and interesting, but they often lack the hardiness and exotic colors of the coral fishes. For this reason and because of their natural habits, they are best placed in a separate tank with others from a similar environment.

Porcupinefishes

This group includes the porcupinefish, burrfish, and balloonfish. They all are covered with sharp spines and have the ability to inflate their bodies by gulping air or water. The spines of the burrfish are permanently erect, while those of the other species stand up only when the fishes assume their balloon-like shape.

Most of the fishes of this family are too large to be kept in the home aquarium. The striped burrfish and the balloonfish, however, make good specimens. They do, however, develop hollow-belly and should be provided with whole or cracked crab, antennas from spiny lobsters, freshwater crayfish, and earthworms.

Puffers

Closely related to the porcupinefishes are the puffers. They lack the sharp spines but are covered with fine prickles that are evident when the puffer puffs up. The puffers are notorious biters and pickers and if placed with other fishes should be given plenty of room. The sharpnose puffer is a pretty little creature that does quite well in captivity. This and the checkered puffer are two of the more attractive members of the family Tetraodontidae.

Trunkfishes and Cowfishes

The trunkfishes and cowfishes possess a hard external shell formed by the fusing and thickening of the scales. In spite of their rigid structure they can move through the water with surprising speed. The cowfishes get their name from the two forward-pointing horns on the head. When excited, many of the trunkfishes exude a poisonous mucus that will kill other fishes in the same container. Very young trunkfishes are known as "beans" and sold under this name.

Atlantic Marine Tropicals

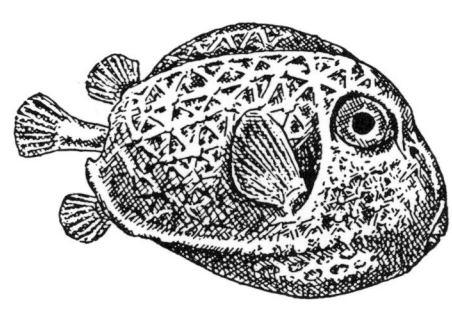

Trunkfish.

Sargassumfish

Well camouflaged, the sargassumfish clambers about its sargassum weed jungle feeding on small fishes, crabs, and shrimp. The prehensile pectoral fins actually grasp the weed as the fish moves about. In an aquarium it has an amazing capacity for gulping down one fish after another, and if several of these species are placed in the same tank it will soon be like the Chinese box, one inside the other, inside the other. This talent, along with its hardiness in aquaria, evidently has made it a marine favorite.

Sea Horses

The various sea horse species have received so much publicity that much curiosity has undoubtedly arisen concerning the possibilities of maintaining and breeding them in home aquaria.

The Florida species most adapted to breeding is *Hippocampus zosterae,* known as the dwarf sea horse, which seldom reaches more than one inch in length. The adults are small enough to be fed newly hatched brine shrimp, which cannot be done in the case of the spotted sea horse. This larger species, when fully matured, usually requires either live *Daphnia,* brine shrimp, or small guppy or minnow fry.

The courtship of *H. zosterae* has been reported by Mr. Dick Boyd of Sarasota, Fla., as a delicate affair in which the male nods, preens, and fans the female, who soon responds in a mating embrace. Later the fertilized eggs are transferred by the female into a pouch located under the stomach of the male. "Pregnant" male sea horses are often collected, and these, along with the tank-bred horses, incubate the eggs for about 10 days. As time for delivery nears the male should be offered a well-cured twig of dead gorgonian skeleton or other inert perching material, onto which he will affix himself, holding fast with the prehensile tail. By shaking, twisting, and rubbing his full pouch, he will attempt to rid himself of the burden. Soon about 20 or 30 babies emerge. These are complete miniatures of the parents and will soon busily be eating brine shrimp. The young mature in two or three months and have a life span of about one year. In water of 85 °F, males hatch about two broods per month, except November through January, during which time no breeding takes place.

Although the newly hatched young of the sea horse do not return to the father's pouch for protection, those of the closely related pipe fish do succeed to some extent in jamming themselves back into the protective cavity in an emergency.

If algae form in the rearing container, they usually afford food for the brine shrimp, which are in turn eaten by the growing sea

Atlantic Marine Tropicals

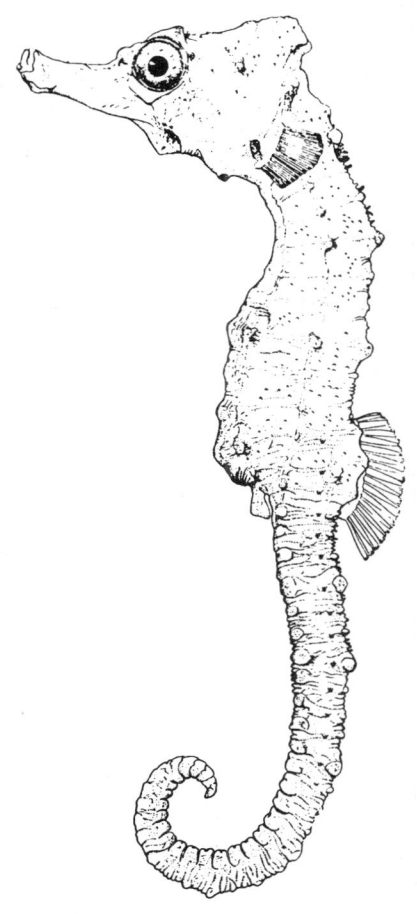

Sea horse, Hippocampus *species.*

growth, but not so much that the water becomes uncomfortably warm.

The newly hatched young of the larger spotted sea horse, numbering over 200 in each brood, although actually smaller than *H. zosterae* of the same age, can be reared on brine shrimp until seven or eight months old. At this time, or soon after, they will require a larger live food as has been suggested before. The babies should be separated from the father, who will eat them, especially if no other food is available.

Miscellaneous Fishes

Quite often a scoop with a net through grass or a seine haul in shallow water will produce a conglomeration of small fishes, difficult to identify because of their size. Among these will be species of tangs, grunts, snappers, filefishes, parrotfishes, and porgies. Some will take hold very well in an aquarium and grow until they must be moved to another tank or returned to the sea. Others will languish and die shortly because of lack of proper food. Many of these small fishes are constantly feeding all day long on algae and minute crustaceans. It is difficult for the aquarist to provide this food.

horses. From all indications it is advisable to permit some direct sunlight to enter the tank each day so that the babies are exposed to ultraviolet light which seems to aid in their

d

Pacific Marine Tropicals

Quite properly perhaps, the title of this chapter should be "Indo-Pacific Marine Tropicals," because many of the fishes that are thought of as coming only from the Pacific Ocean have ranges that include parts of the Indian Ocean as well. A few range into the Red Sea. Some species, for example the longnose butterflyfish, are distributed all the way from the east coast of Africa to the Hawaiian Islands or even to the Western Pacific. So the fishes included in this chapter are to be found in the great body of water stretching from Africa eastward to the western coast of the Americas.

Among the Pacific marine tropicals we find representatives of many of the same families that occur in the Atlantic. The butterflyfishes, wrasses, gobies, blennies, and damselfishes are but a few. Even within families there are common genera such as *Chaetodon, Centropyge, Thalassoma, Abudefduf,* and others. There are, however, few if any species common to both the Atlantic and Pacific Oceans that would come to the attention of the home aquarist. You can be reasonably sure, therefore, that any fishes shipped in from the Pacific area will be new and different from any Atlantic species previously kept.

Obviously it would be impossible in the limited scope of this chapter to mention all the Pacific fishes that are suited for small aquariums. Some will be overlooked purposely, some unintentionally, but it is hoped that a good representative selection of the fishes of this area will be presented here.

Angelfishes and Butterflyfishes

Like their Florida and Bahama counterparts, the Pacific angelfishes and butterflyfishes are among the most beautiful on the reefs. Ranging in size from little fellows of two or three inches to moderate-sized fish of two feet, they display an almost endless variety of colors and patterns. As if one beautiful display weren't enough during a lifetime, many of these individuals go through color and pattern changes as they mature. The result in many cases is that the adult coloration is even more striking than the juvenile.

Three angelfishes that have attained great popularity with home aquarists are the Koran, the imperial, and the blue-ring. The first gets its name from a specimen that appeared in the market in Zanzibar. Markings on the tail fin bore resemblance to old Arabic characters, which read, on one side of the tail—*Laillaha Illalah* (There is no God but Allah), and on the other side—*Shani-Allah* (a warning sent from Allah). These two phrases are supposedly quotes from the Koran, the book of scriptures of the Mohammedans. The fish that originally sold for a penny eventually brought 5000 rupees.

The young of these species are quite similar, which has led to considerable confusion in their identification and classification. This is further complicated by the above-mentioned color changes that occur with growth. Each color phase has, at some time or another, been named as a separate species. The young

41

are for the most part dark blue crossed with white and light blue lines. In the emperor angelfish *(Pomacanthus imperator)* the light line nearest the tail forms a complete ring and the successive preceding lines are less and less curved until those on the head are practically vertical. There are about 15 of these lines, which increase as the fish grows to 25 yellow bands running obliquely upwards and backwards from a black patch above the pectoral fin. This change takes place at a length of about four inches. The change in the Koran angelfish *(Pomacanthus semicirculatus)* is just as dramatic, but the adult coloration is less spectacular. In this species, alternately broad and narrow backward-curving semicircular lines give way with age to a general spotting and then to the final adult stage in which the fish is yellowish anteriorly, grayish-brown towards the rear, and spotted irregularly over the sides. The young of the blue-ring *(Pomacanthus annularis)* exhibit a pattern similar to the other two species. The adult is yellowish brown with a blue ring on the shoulder and six or seven curved blue bands running from the pectoral to the dorsal fin. In addition there are two horizontal blue stripes on the head, one passing through the eye and the other below it.

These angelfishes seem to be less hardy than the Atlantic species. They do not eat as readily and seem to have a shorter lifespan in the aquarium, but there are of course individuals that will prove to be exceptions. Their favorite food is live adult brine shrimp, and this should be fed if at all possible. After the fish is established and feeding well, a shift to a less expensive and more readily available food can be attempted.

The blackstripe angelfish *(Apolemichthys arcuatus)* is restricted to the Hawaiian Islands. It is a handsome species, all white with a single broad dark band running horizontally through the eye and arching slightly upward to the last rays of the dorsal fin. It would be difficult to confuse this with any other species. This fish grows to about seven or eight inches, but smaller specimens are obtainable. As it is one of the more difficult species to keep it is not recommended for the beginner.

From the west coast of tropical America comes the Cortez angelfish *(Pomacanthus zonipectus)*. It is similar to the Atlantic French angelfish but generally brighter and more colorful. It has touches of blue on the dorsal, anal, and pelvic fins.

The regal angelfish *(Pygoplites diacanthus)* is all that its name implies. It is a strikingly beautiful fish, basically yellow-orange. This coloration is interrupted by seven or eight broad vertical bright blue bands, each edged in black.

Some of the most satisfactory aquarium specimens are the pygmy angelfishes. These fishes grow to about four inches and get along well with both larger and smaller specimens of their own and other species. Potter's angelfish *(Centropyge potteri)* has russet and blue vertical barring on the body, with russet predominating anteriorly and dorsally, blue predominating posteriorly and ventrally. The tail is completely dark blue. The lemon peel *(Centropyge flavissimus)*, another of the pygmy angels, is a brilliant chrome yellow with a bright blue ring around the eye and a short vertical blue line on the gill cover. In addition, young specimens show an ocellated blue spot on the middle of the side. The bi-color cherub is reminiscent of the Atlantic rock beauty. The front half of the fish and the tail are bright yellow, while the back half, up to the tail, is a very deep blue. Feedings with live and frozen brine shrimp should be alternated with chopped clams and shrimp and a good dried food mix.

The number of butterflyfishes from the Indo-Pacific area is almost legion. Many are extremely colorful, many are drab. Some do well in aquariums, while others seem to resist all attempts to keep them alive. Unless one is an experienced aquarist it is not a good idea to try to keep any but the more hardy species.

The raccoon and the threadfin butterflyfishes *(Chaetodan lunula* and *Chaetodon auriga)* are two species that are relatively easy to keep. They eagerly take live and frozen brine shrimp and will adapt to cut food such as chopped shrimp and clams. Algae should be fed if available, alone or mixed with the shrimp. In nature, butterflyfishes are constantly nibbling and picking for food, as are many other small marine fishes. It is desirable, therefore, to feed small amounts of food often rather than give them single large meals.

The raccoon butterfly is easily recognized by its overall orangish color and the broad bold black bands, one of which passes through the eyes and across the snout like a bandit's mask. Immediately in back of this is an equally broad white band. From this white band, at the angle of the gill cover, a very broad black band runs up and back to the dorsal fin. The effect is to give the fish a raccoon-like appearance. The filament butterfly is characterized by a black bar through the eye, an oval black spot on the dorsal fin rays, two sets of oblique dark lines set at right angles to one another, and the dorsal fin tapers off to a filament. Other members of this family that are imported frequently are the milletseed *(Chaetodon miliaris)*, bluestripe *(Chaetodon fremblii)*, red-tailed *(Chaetodon collare)*, saddleback *(Chaetodon ephippium)*, teardrop *(Chaetodon unimaculatus)*, and Klein's *(Chaetodon kleinii)* butterflies. Of these the red-tailed is the hardiest and certainly one of the prettiest. Varying degrees of success have been met in keeping the others, but usually after one of these fishes is eating well and established in a tank it will live for a considerable length of time.

Two common butterflyfish species masquerade under the name of longnose butterflyfish. One of them is the perennial favorite *Forcipger flavissimus*, and the other is *Chelmon rostratus*. To avoid confusion the latter is now called the copperband butterfly or by its generic name, as is the practice for many of our aquarium fishes. In Hawaii the longnose butterfly is called *lau-wiliwili-nukunuku-ʻoi-ʻoi,* which, literally translated, means "an unpredictable fish with a long, long nose." The extended snout of this species and *Chelmon* is especially well adapted for picking up small invertebrates from deep within cracks and crevices. The longnose, especially, uses its long dorsal spines for defense and fighting. It can be induced to eat live food and does quite well in aquariums.

Chelmon is a strikingly marked and colored fish. Five copper-orange stripes stand out against a silver background. The first of these passes through the eye while the last passes across the caudal peduncle from the soft dorsal to the anal rays. A black ocellated spot is located high on the broad fourth stripe. Again, for this species, live food is best, and the usual brine shrimp can be alternated with *Tubifex,* white worms, and blood worms.

Another favorite with aquarists is *Heniochus acuminatus,* the pennant or banner butterflyfish. Although it is known by this common name, it is commonly known also as simply *Heniochus.* It can be recognized at once by the broad black and white banding on the sides and the elongated fourth dorsal spine, which streams backward like a banner. In addition, it has some yellow on the soft dorsal and caudal fins. Specimens smaller than three inches acclimate nicely to aquarium conditions, but the larger ones do not stand shipping and the change of environment. Small *Heniochus* will eat both live and frozen brine shrimp and can be coaxed to take dried food. They are quite peaceful and get along well with other fishes.

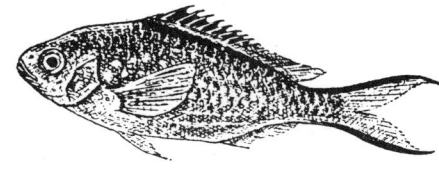

Chromis marginatus, *one of the damselfishes.*

Moorish Idols

Probably one of the most sought after and most beautiful and bizarre, but unfortunately one of the most difficult to keep fishes is the Moorish idol, or kihikihi. The Moorish idol is a member of the family Zanclidae and is closely related to the surgeonfishes.

This is an extremely common fish in Hawaii and prefers quiet waters. It apparently can withstand considerable pollution and salinity changes, as it can be seen in the murky waters of Honolulu harbor swimming and feeding actively. It is discouraging to remove a fish from such a habitat, give it the best of conditions, and then have it die, apparently killed with kindness. Occasionally, however, a small specimen will take nicely to the aquarium and will feed on brine shrimp and algae. Because it seems to be constantly feeding, a certain amount of algae should be allowed to accumulate in its tank so it can browse at will. This fish is relatively expensive, and the novice should not attempt to keep it unless the loss of such a specimen is of no financial consequence.

Stripey

Occasionally we are fortunate to find a fish that possesses most, if not all, of the qualities desirable in an aquarium fish. Such a species is the stripey *(Microcanthus strigatus)*. The stripey is marked with black and yellow-gold horizontal stripes. It is an active fish, constantly on the move; it eats well and takes almost any food offered. It adapts nicely to aquarium conditions, is not timid, and gets along well with other fishes. Although not imported in any great quantity it is available at fairly reasonable prices.

Damselfishes

Fishes of this family are usually small, colorful hardy fishes of the reef and include, among others, the genera *Amphiprion, Dascyllus, Chromis, Pomacentrus,* and *Abudefduf.*

The members of the genus *Amphiprion* are known collectively as anemonefishes. They live in relationship with large anemones such as *Stoichactis* and *Discosoma.* While other small fishes may be killed by the stinging cells (nematocysts) of the anemone, the anemonefishes can swim in and out of the tentacles without harm. It was discovered in 1958 by Drs. Demorest Davenport and Kenneth Norris that the anemonefish gives off a mucus that prevents the anemone from discharging its nematocysts.

For a long time it was believed that this relationship was a one-sided affair, that the fish received protection and gave nothing in return. However, the fishes have been observed bringing food to the anemones and also "treating" them in some manner by rubbing against them and picking at their stalks and tentacles. In the aquarium, without a fish as a companion, some anemones eventually waste away and die. This relationship, where both members of the association receive benefit, is a symbiotic arrangement called mutualism.

To distinguish the old orange and white standby, *Amphiprion ocellarius,* from the rest of the anemone fishes that eventually appeared on the market, *ocellaris* was given the nickname clown anemonefish, which gradually degenerated to clownfish and then to just plain clown. This gradually led to many, if not all, of the anemonefishes' being called clowns, and they in turn have been given identifying adjectival names in order to distinguish one from the other. So we find ourselves in the position of having a perfectly good and descriptive name replaced by one that for many members of the group is meaningless. There may be some basis for calling *A. ocellaris* the clown anemonefish because of its gaudy clown-like costume, but nothing could be more undescriptive than names such as pink skunk clown, orange skunk clown, tomato, two-stripe tomato, brown, and maroon clown. There is nothing clown-like at all about a pale pink fish with a light stripe along the base of the dorsal fin. To make matters worse, fishes of a completely unrelated family are known as clownfishes; for example, the "chocolate polka dot clownfish," *Plectorhynchus chaetodonoides,* one of the sweetlips.

Anemonefishes, then, should be used for the major identifying common name of the fishes of this genus, and there is nothing wrong in retaining the present adjectival names.

When several anemonefishes are kept in a tank with their commensal anemone *Discosoma.* the most aggressive will take over the anemone and keep the other fishes away. When this dominant fish dies or is removed, his place is taken by the next man on the totem pole. This does not seem to be the case, however, when *Stoichactis* is involved. Specimens of this anemone have been seen with as many as two dozen clown anemonefish nestled among their tentacles. Whether this holds true in nature is not known.

The fishes that are imported today under the name of tomato anemonefish, which for years were known by the very descriptive name of glowing coal fish, belong to several species, including *Amphiprion ephippium* and *A. melanopus.*

The saddleback anemonefish *(Amphiprion polymnus)* is brown with a broad white band on the head and an even broader white saddle mark on the upper side and soft dorsal fin. The orange anemonefish *(Amphiprion sandaracinos)* has a narrow white band from the snout along the base of the dorsal fin to the caudal peduncle. The pink anemonefish *(Amphiprion perideraion)* has a narrow white band on top of the head and a narrow white vertical bar on the side of the head behind the eye. Clark's anemonefish *(Amphiprion clarkii)* has three white bars on a brown background.

One other ought to be mentioned, the maroon anemonefish *(Premnas biaculeatus).* Its usual color is, as its name implies, maroon, with three equally spaced white vertical bands that are edged with black. This fish can be recognized by the two strong spines below the eye. In larger specimens the upper one may reach to the first white band.

Fishes of the genus *Dascyllus* are usually found in large groups, often hovering around a coral head or steep coral face. At a sign of danger they will dive into the spaces between the fingers of coral or into small holes in rocks from which it is impossible to get them except by breaking the coral apart. Attempts to pull them out result only in injuring the fish, for they flare their gill covers and erect their dorsal and anal spines, forming a very effective anchoring mechanism.

In an aquarium they are likely to be quite bossy, so care must be taken as to

Pacific Marine Tropicals

which fishes are introduced into their tank. It is sometimes best to remove these pomacentrids for a few days or separate them with a piece of glass. These fishes are voracious eaters and relish a diet of brine shrimp, the freshwater crustacean *Gammarus, Tubifex*, algae, and perhaps spinach or kale if algae is not available.

Species regularly appearing on the market are the humbug *(Dascyllus aruanus)*, the three-spot or domino *(Dascyllus trimaculatus)*, the black-tail *(Dascyllus melanurus)*, and the Hawaiian dascyllus *(Dascyllus albisella)*.

Damselfishes of the genera *Abudefduf* and *Pomacentrus* are hardy in the aquarium but apt to be a bit scrappy. They should be kept with fishes that are as close to their size as possible. Many of these grow large and unless provided with enough room will soon outgrow their quarters. The species known as "devils" are probably the most popular of this group, with the most common being the blue devil and neon damsels. The color of the blue devil *(Chrysiptera cyanea)* varies from navy blue to deep sky blue with numerous light dots. When the fish is excited these dots turn dark. The neon devil *(Pomacentris coelestris)* is almost an iridescent blue. Green shrimp, beef, brine shrimp, and algae or lettuce should be included in their diet.

A very hardy little fish from Hawaii is the kupipi, or black spot sergeant *(Abudefduf sordidus)*. It has the general shape of the Atlantic sergeant major and can be distinguished from similar Hawaiian species by the black spot at the rear base of the soft dorsal and a light yellow blotch on the spiny dorsal. This active little fish is found in tide and surge pools along with young island perch, rock skippers, and gobies.

An attractive pomacentrid from our southern California coast is the garibaldi *(Hypsypops rubicunda)*. The adults grow to about a foot in length and are quite chunky fish. Specimens more than two and one-half to three inches long are a brilliant orange, but individuals smaller than this are spotted and blotched with blue. Like most damsels, they tend to be peppery and should have plenty of room and places to hide.

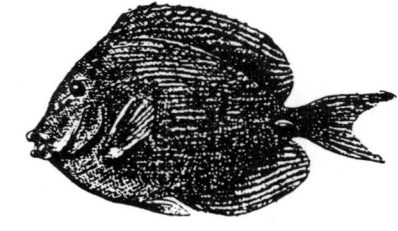

Blue tang, Acanthurus caeruleus.

Wrasses

The Indo-Pacific provides us with beautiful and hardy members of this family. As with the angelfishes, many members of this family change color and pattern as they mature. Many wrasses bury themselves in the sand at night. The examples given here are mostly Hawaiian.

Pacific Marine Tropicals

The saddle wrasse *(Thalassoma duperreyi)* is a blue-green fish, the color more intense on the head and less so on the body. Immediately in back of the head is a broad russet-brown saddle, from dorsal to ventral midlines. This is the most common wrasse in Hawaii, being found in almost every type of habitat. It reaches a length of about a foot, but is commonly seen at five to six inches. Although an attractive addition to a tank, it has the nasty habit of fighting with members of its own species. Using its long canine teeth, it can neatly nip fins or remove the eyes of its tankmates.

In heavy surge areas, close to rocks, the green wrasse *(Thalassoma purpureum)* can often be caught on hook and line using small shrimp, or *opai,* for bait. This is an attractive little fish, always on the move. The basic color is green with black vertical markings that form rectangles. Another species carries almost the same pattern, but its ground color is orange with green rectangles.

An especially hardy member of this family is *Thalassoma ballieui,* the wrinkled wrasse or *hinalea luahine* (hin-ah-LAY-ah loo-ah-HEE-nee). In Hawaiian *hinalea* is the general name for all wrasses and *luahine* means "old lady." The basic color of this fish is light tan, each scale carrying a thin dark vertical mark or dash that gives the fish a wrinkled appearance. This supposedly gave rise to its native name.

The twinspot wrasse *(Coris aygula)* displays a startling color pattern. The fish is light gray or white with the front half of the body as well as the dorsal and anal fins speckled with small dark spots. Two large black and red oval spots dominate the rear half of the fish and give the appearance of two very tired, droopy, and bloodshot eyes.

The young of *hinalea lolo,* the clown wrasse *(Coris gaimardi),* was once thought to be a separate species. Study of a series of specimens by Dr. Leonard P. Schultz of the U.S. National Museum proved without a doubt that this species goes through a series of color changes as it matures. Young specimens are bright orange-red with five black-bordered white patches on the upper sides. The first of these is on the snout and the last on the caudal peduncle. The adult is a veritable rainbow of colors. The body is reddish-brown covered with small bright blue spots that are more numerous toward the rear. The dull red head has a blue line through and above the eye, and green lines behind and below the eye and under the head. The dorsal and anal fins are reddish with blue spots at their bases and blue streaks toward the edges. All of this is terminated with a bright yellow tail.

The young are found in shallow waters around coral heads, but the adults move out into deeper water. This fish has a wide range, but it is not plentiful in any one place. The young do well in aquaria and as they are constantly feeding should be given a constant supply of live food and algae. This fish is reputed to be a snail-eater.

Some of the labrids have long beaks. That of the birds wrasse *(Gomphosus varius*) is the longest, and it uses this flexible proboscis for poking into nooks and crannies in search of food. The dark green males and brown females were once thought to be separate species, but studies indicate these are sexual color variations.

One of the strangest relationships in the ocean is that of the cleaner fishes and their hosts. Many species of fishes are known to pick parasites and fungi from other fishes, and in addition there are shrimp, crabs, and a worm that provide this service. The cleaner wrasses (*Labroides dimidiatus*) are well known for this phenomenon and if placed in a tank with larger fishes can occasionally be seen performing their duties. A wolf in sheep's clothing is a sharp-toothed little blenny (*Aspidontus*), which imitates the livery of the cleaner wrasses. Posing as a friend in need it approaches the unsuspecting host and takes a bite, usually from the gills.

Groupers

The groupers, with few exceptions, have not gained wide acceptance as home aquarium fishes. For the most part they grow too large and will eat anything in the tank that moves. The most popular fish of this family is the golden stripe grouper (*Grammistes sexlineatus*). This fish is dark brown or black with gold or yellow stripes. In very young specimens (one-half inch) there are only two stripes made up of a series of dots. As the fish grows the number of stripes increases to as many as 12 or 15. These are not all complete stripes and one or more may be present on one side and not on the other. The golden stripe grouper is a particularly hardy species in captivity and will eat cut fish and beef or horse meat. It grows to about 10 inches; it is recommended that this fish be kept by itself or with other fishes too large to be swallowed whole.

Cardinalfishes

Although the name of this family suggests a group of bright red-hued fishes, many are quite dull and colored other than red. Some are striped red and yellow, red and green, and black and white. Others are basically green, brown, or bronze. Some are almost nondescript. The mouths of these fishes are large and they are oral incubators, the males carrying the eggs. With their large mouths they are capable of swallowing smaller aquarium fishes. There are many species of cardinalfishes, chiefly shallow-water marine forms. Most of them are delicate and do poorly in captivity, but there are exceptions, such as the fish being imported under the name angel wings.

Sweetlips

The sweeplips are pretty little fishes, some quite gaudily marked. There is considerable disagreement as to their classification. They fall somewhere between the grunts (Pomadasydae) and the snappers (Lutianidae). Authors place them in one or the other of these families, or in a family of their own. There is even disagreement as to whether this family name should be Gaterinidae or Plectorhynchidae. For our purposes, this is a little academic. The main thing is that they make a welcome addition to marine tanks. Dr. Earl S. Herald considered them as the clowns of the reef because their fluttering swimming motion looks like the cavorting of clowns.

This is another group of fishes the colors of which change with growth. The younger ones are more gaudy and of course a better size for aquariums. Some of the most popular of this family are the clown or polka dot sweetlips (*Plectorhynchus chaetodonoides*), the yellow-banded (*P. lineatus*), and the Oriental sweetlips (*P. orientalis*). The first is cocoa brown with large irregular white patches. The second is a yellowish-white fish, usually with six dark brown horizontal bands of varying width. The last is irregularly marked with bands and patches of yellow and chestnut. The sweetlips are rather delicate fishes. They should be handled with care and given considerable variety in their diet. Various members of this family range from the Red Sea and east coast of Africa through the Indian Ocean to the East Indies, Australia, Philippines, and islands of the South Pacific.

Blennies and Gobies

The blennies and gobies are frequently confused by the uninitiated and it is no wonder, because the fishes of these two families resemble each other in size, shape, coloration, and habit. Many are found in tide or surge pools, over sand bottoms, in holes in the silt, or in cracks in the coral and rock. Most of these fishes are drab, blending in well with their sand or rock background, but some are quite colorful.

The gobies in general have a separate first dorsal fin composed of six spines and the two pelvic fins are fused to form a sucking disc. The blennies have a single dorsal fin, which may be almost, but not completely, divided by a deep notch. They are also characterized by their pelvic fins, which are jugular in position and have two to four rays.

All of these fishes are seemingly quite pert and inquisitive. If one swims over a reef or silt bottom or disturbs a tide pool, blennies and gobies will scatter like popcorn, diving for their holes like a colony of prairie dogs. Within seconds, however, heads begin to reappear to take a second look at the intruder. If no further disturbance is made these little fellows will emerge and go about their endless business of feeding on minute crustaceans, algae, and detritus. Perched atop a rock or coral head, propped on their fins, they look like lords of all they survey.

One of the most famous of the blennies is the rock skipper, or zebra blenny. It inhabits spray and tide pools that are subject to considerable heating and evaporation in the hot tropical sun, and also to sudden cooling and dilution by rain squalls. Therefore, these blennies must be able to withstand a wide range of temperature and salinity. Their leaps from pool to pool are extremely accurate and well timed. They seem to know the location of several escape routes and do a good job of making their pursuers look foolish. The best method of capturing them is to close off their escape route with a hand net and "tickle" them out of their holes with a stiff wire. When they come flopping out they usually take a leap right into the net. The rock skipper's name is *Istiblennius zebra.*

Blennies are best displayed in a shallow tank with rocks both above and below the water line. They will provide a lot of amusement hopping back and forth over the rocks from one puddle to another.

The rock skipper can be distinguished from other Hawaiian blennies by the fleshy crest on the mid-line of the head, although blennies from other areas of the Pacific have a similar crest.

The golden blenny *(Meiacanthus atrodorsalis oualanensis)* is probably one of the most attractive of the blennies. It is active and graceful and in our experience gets along well with other fishes. It is a uniform bright yellow and has a large lyre-shaped caudal fin. It feeds on *Artemia,* small bits of beef, and shellfish. Two large canine teeth in the lower jaw and two smaller ones in the upper are used to advantage in removing small snails from their shells.

The mud skippers *(Periophthalmus* species) are some of the most interesting

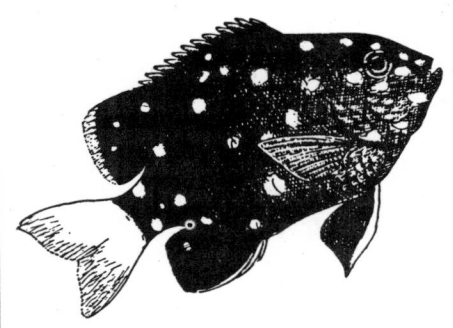

Marine jewelfish, Microspathodon chrysurus.

of the gobies. They are found from Africa to Oceania, living on mud flats and in mangrove swamps. Like the rock skippers, they are adapted for traveling across land almost faster than a man can move. If the skin and gills are kept moist they can remain out of water for quite some time. Their large pop-eyes and their habit of supporting themselves on their pectoral fins give them an inquisitive mien.

These little fishes become quite tame and will respond at feeding time by rushing to their food like a litter of puppies. Chunks of frozen brine shrimp or a pile of ground beef will be greedily attacked.

From Catalina Island off the coast of California comes one of the most beautiful gobies. The blue-banded—or Catalina—goby *(Lythrypnus dalli)* is a fairly small fish, averaging about two inches in length. It is red-orange, with five or six narrow violet-blue bands on the sides. This fish is very common at depths below 20 feet, living in cracks and holes in the rocks. This habit, plus the fact that it seems to be loath to flee, makes it easy to capture with a slurp gun.

This fish feeds readily on larval *Artemia,* but fully grown adults are too large. Smaller *Artemia* obtained by sifting the shrimp through cheesecloth or bolting cloth are satisfactory. The blue-banded goby does best if kept in water no warmer than 65 °F.

Scorpionfishes or Lionfishes

There are several lionfish species regularly imported, the most common of which is *Pterois volitans,* variously called lionfish, turkeyfish, scorpionfish, etc. This is a spectacular and handsome species, as are all members of its genus. Other species that are seen occasionally are the spotfin lionfish, the clearfin, and the Hawaiian lionfish. Although all of these species appear quite similar at first glance, there are considerable differences. The lionfish has at least 15 vertical bands on the head and body that are as wide or wider than the pupil of the eye. These broader bands alternate with narrower and lighter ones. The spotfin lionfish *(Pterois antennata)* has fewer but broader bands, about eight in number, again alternated with narrower ones. In addition, the membranes of the pectoral fins are spotted with larger dots toward the bases and smaller dots toward the extremities. The clearfin lionfish *(Pterois radiata),* which has no spots on the

pectorals, has the reddish-brown of its sides interrupted by very fine Y-shaped white lines and two horizontal white lines on the caudal peduncle. The Hawaiian lionfish *(Pterois sphex)* is banded like the spotfin but its color is more reddish and it lacks the pectoral spots. This latter species is restricted to Hawaii.

The dwarf lionfishes are rather drab in comparison to their larger cousins, but show the same general color pattern. They are more common than *Pterois,* and small specimens are frequently found on the underside of rocks and coral in shallow water. The dwarf lionfishes *(Dendrochirus* spp.) can be separated from the lionfishes *(Pterois* spp.) by the upper pectoral rays. Those of *Dendrochirus* are branched and do not extend beyond the membranes, whereas those of *Pterois* are simple and frequently project as free filaments.

All of these fishes are quite dangerous because of the venomous nature of the dorsal, anal, and ventral spines. While no deaths have been reported from their stings, the pain is excruciating. Victims have been known to writhe uncontrollably and beat the affected member on the ground. Others run, sit, lie down, and get up and run again, apparently not knowing how to get relief. Some faint and go into shock. The best relief from this pain comes from immersion of the injured in hot water and from injections of novocaine or emetine hydrochloride.

These fishes are very hardy in aquaria. However, it is difficult to induce them to eat anything but live food. When given large guppies or small goldfish they stalk their food until within several inches; then, with a powerful thrust of their fins, they make a short, fast lunge and swallow their prey whole.

In view of their potential danger, these fishes are not recommended for a household where small children are present.

Tangs or Surgeonfishes

The fishes of this family (Acanthuridae) are characterized either by a single movable spine that folds forward into a groove or by several fixed spines at the base of the tail. These spines are capable of producing a deep gash, and consequently these fishes should be handled with care. One species, *Naso lituratus,* has been known to charge swimmers and divers, in some cases inflicting painful wounds.

For the most part the tangs are herbivorous and constantly graze algae. Most of them will eat other foods in captivity, such as ground fresh shrimp and adult *Artemia,* but languish and die unless their diet is supplemented with algae.

One of the best known and most beautiful of these fishes is the yellow tang (*Zebrasoma flavescens*). It is a bright clear yellow except for the caudal spine, which is white. When excited or scared, a white streak appears on the sides, extending backwards from the pectoral fins. This fish grows to a length of eight inches, but specimens four to five inches are most commonly seen.

The sailfin tang (*Zebrasoma veliferum*) is closely related to the yellow tang. It possesses extremely large dorsal and anal fins, from which it gets its name. The sailfin prefers quiet waters and does not seem to be as common as the yellow tang. Smaller specimens do fairly well in tanks, but they are not among the most hardy aquarium fishes. Like the yellow tang, this fish should be provided with plenty of algae. It is found from the Western Pacific to Hawaii.

The most abundant of the Hawaiian tangs is the convict tang or *manini* (*Acanthurus triostegus sandvicensis*). Although a closely related subspecies is found from Africa to Baja California, this form is restricted to Hawaiian waters. This is a silvery gray fish with five black bars, the first of which passes through the eye. Like the other tangs, the manini should be fed algae along with green shrimp and *Artemia.*

Triggerfishes, Filefishes, Boxfishes and Puffers

Although these fishes have little external resemblance to each other, skeletally they are quite similar. They are placed in the order Plectognathi, along with the ocean sunfishes, on the basis of the structure of the jaws, the reduction of the gill openings, and elongation of the pelvic bones. Fishes of this group also show reduction and loss of ventral and spinous dorsal fins, specialization,

Pacific Marine Tropicals

reduction, and loss of scales, and fusion of the teeth in the upper jaw.

The triggerfishes are comparatively slow swimmers. When approached underwater they give an alarm or warning signal consisting of a series of quite rapid and quite audible grunts. If this fails to discourage the pursuer, they enter a hole and raise their stout first dorsal spine, locking themselves in place. To get them out it is necessary to trip the trigger mechanism by depressing the smaller second spine making it possible to lower the first.

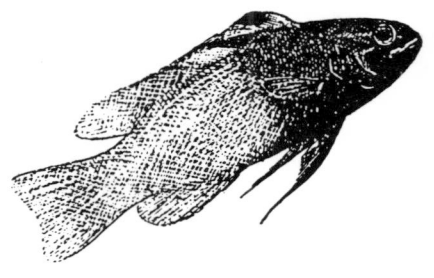

Royal gramma, Gramma loretto.

These fishes are some of the most spectacular residents of the reef. The blue and gold undulate triggerfish *(Balistes undulatus)* and the spotted triggerfish *(Balistoides conspicillum),* with its white polka dots and red lips, are almost beyond comparison. Most of these species are too large for the home aquarium, and many are expensive.

Probably the best known triggerfish is the *humuhumu-nukunuku-a-pua'a,* which has the distinction of being one of the few fishes mentioned in the lyrics of a song, the song being *I Want to Go Back to My Little Grass Shack in Kealakekua, Hawaii.* It can be distinguished from all other triggerfishes by the forward-pointing black wedge on the caudal peduncle. Other species are the black or blueline triggerfish *(Melichthys niger),* which is also found in the tropical Atlantic, and the pinktail triggerfish *(Melichthys vidua)*—a black fish with transparent fins and a pink tail.

These fishes will eat almost anything—cut fish, shrimp, crabs, clams—all are attacked with gusto.

The filefishes are quite similar to the triggerfishes but can be recognized by their velvety skin, thinner bodies, and the position of the dorsal spine. In the filefishes this spine is over the eye, whereas in the triggerfishes it is behind the eye. Not many filefishes are imported, perhaps because of their drab coloration. However, several species are quite beautiful. One of these, the fantail filefish, *(Pervagor spilosoma)* is yellow with many black spots covering the sides. Its spectacular tail is orange with a black border. This is usually carried folded, but when the fish's territory is threatened the tail is spread into an almost perfect half circle and the dorsal spine is erected. With this display, two of these "bantam roosters" will circle each other or jockey back and forth in a head to tail position, each trying to outbluff the other, and all the while rapidly vibrating their dorsal spines.

From the waters of Samoa and Fiji and west to the East Indies comes a fantastic little fish. This is the orangespotted filefish *(Oxymonacanthus longirostris)*. Although the color plate in *The Fishes of Samoa* shows it as green with orange spots, the description by Jordan and Seale of the living fish is "sky blue with rows of bright orange spots." The caudal fin is yellow-brown, and the dorsal spine and long snout are orange. At the end of this snout is a small upturned mouth with projecting teeth. Apparently this surrealistic fish spends a good deal of its time picking very small crustaceans and bits of algae from the sides and undersides of rocks and coral.

The scrawled filefish *(Aluterus scriptus)*, found in all tropical seas, grows to gigantic proportions. Specimens as large as 40 inches have been reported. Very small individuals, six to eight inches long, can be kept in home aquaria but should be in a tank of their own. Their razor-sharp triangular teeth are often used to remove bits of fin and flesh from their tankmates. Small live fishes such as guppies and goldfish, or ground fresh shrimp, should be fed.

The boxfishes and cowfishes are not very satisfactory aquarium specimens. Despite their hard shells they are delicate fishes and easily injured. Moreover, they are difficult to feed. One species, the blue trunkfish *(Ostracion lentiginosus)*, is mentioned here because of its interest to science. This fish gives off a poisonous mucus from its mouth when alarmed. This apparently affects the gills of not only other species but the trunkfish as well. Just one of these piscine Lucrezia Borgias in a container as large as a washtub is enough to kill all the fish in it. When caught in a trap and lifted out of the water the fish foams at the mouth like a mad dog.

The little sharpnose puffers *(Canthigaster* spp.) are popular with marine hobbyists. Although colorful, active, and good feeders, they are apt to be a little quarrelsome. These fishes have the peculiar habit of curving their tail forward to either side when swimming slowly with their pectoral fins or when maintaining a stationary position.

The whitespotted puffer *(Canthigaster jactator)* is the most common as well as the smallest of the Hawaiian puffers. Very pale green spots on the head and white spots on the body over a brown ground color identify this species.

The saddle puffer *(Canthigaster valentini)* is variously described as having two, three, or four dark saddle marks. The two largest over the back and down the sides are quite prominent, while those over the eye and the caudal peduncle are smaller and may have been disregarded by some authors. The rest of the fish is light tan or whtie with orange spots.

The bluespotted puffer *(Canthigaster bennetti)* is quite attractive and generally larger than the other two species. This fish is dark above with blue spots and light below with dark brown spots. Dark brown lines run forward and down below the eye, while blue lines radiate from the eye.

These fish enjoy both live and frozen adult brine shrimp and seem to subsist very well on this diet.

Miscellaneous Fishes

Batfishes of the genus *Platax* are among the most handsome and majestic of marine imports. The dorsal and anal fins of young *Platax* are extremely long. A two-inch fish would have fins measuring seven inches between tips. These fins shorten proportionately as the fish grows. The coloration is light brown or gray with three dark vertical stripes, the first through the eye, the second through the base of the pectoral, and the third across the body and fins just in front of the caudal peduncle.

These fishes eat well in captivity, but it may take a little coaxing to get them started. Live brine shrimp and bloodworms are favorite foods.

Several species of batfishes have been described, the most beautiful being the orange-rimmed batfish that as a juvenile is jet black with an orange trim.

The scats (*Scatophagus* spp.), although considered brackish water species, are primarily marine. There are about four or five species widely scattered in the Indo-Pacific. They are greenish gray to yellowish with many large round dark spots. Young specimens of this species have an orange-red coloration on the dorsal surface.

These are very hardy fishes that eat well and soon outgrow a small tank. Cut fish, shrimp, and strips of beef or liver are taken eagerly. They grow to about 12 inches.

The silver batfishes, or moonfishes (*Monodactylus* spp.), are beautiful spade-shaped fishes. They are found in salt, brackish, and fresh water throughout the tropical Indo-Pacific area and the west coast of tropical Africa. They do well in captivity, either in fresh or salt water, growing to about six inches.

The archerfish (*Toxotes jaculator*) is well known for its ability to knock insects into the water with a well-directed stream of water. Perhaps its accuracy has been

P. 57: Saddleback butterflyfish, Chaetodon ephippium. *P. 58, upper photo: Rusty angelfish,* Centropyge ferrugatus; *lower photo: Lyretail coralfish,* Anthias squamipinnis. *P. 59: Copper-band butterflyfish,* Chelmon rostratus. *P. 60: Young blue-girdled angelfish,* Euxiphipops navarchus. *Pp. 60-61: Black-and-white dascyllus,* Dascyllus aruanus. *P. 62, upper photo: Gray angelfish,* Pomacanthus arcuatus; *lower photo: Emperor, or imperial, angelfish,* Pomacanthus imperator. *P. 63: Pennant bannerfish,* Heniochus acuminatus. *P. 64: Young (upper photo) and adult (lower photo) of the coney,* Epinephelus fulvus.

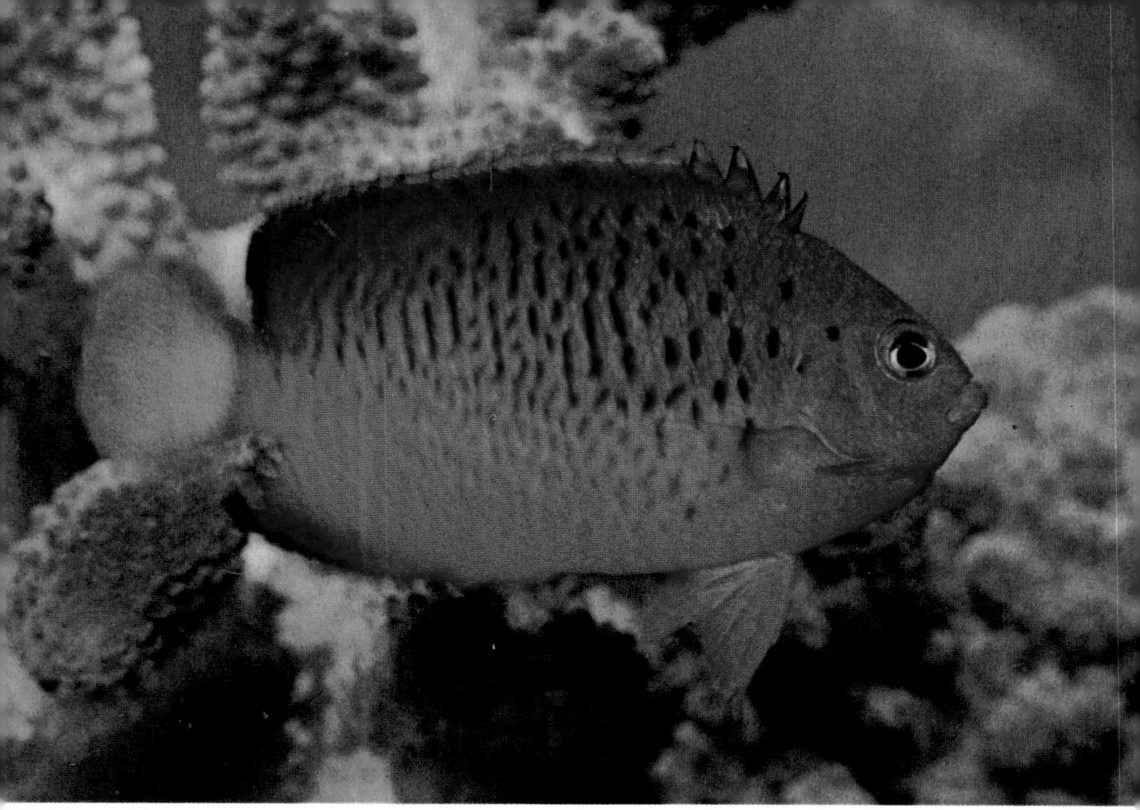

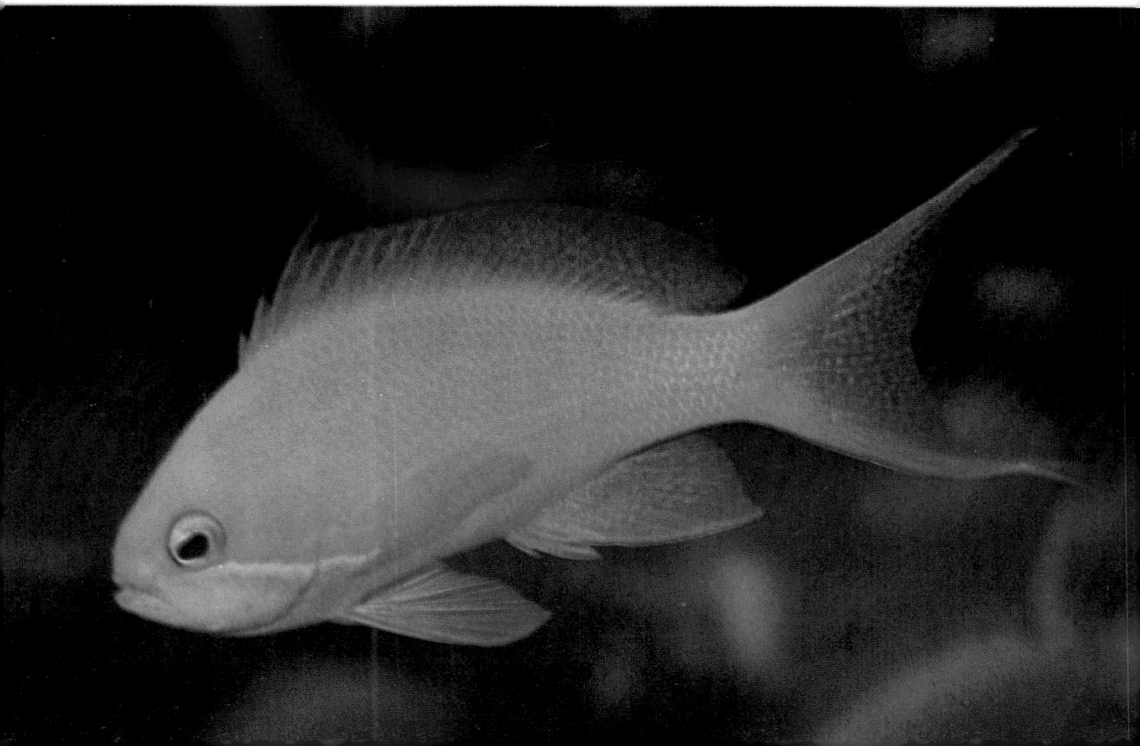

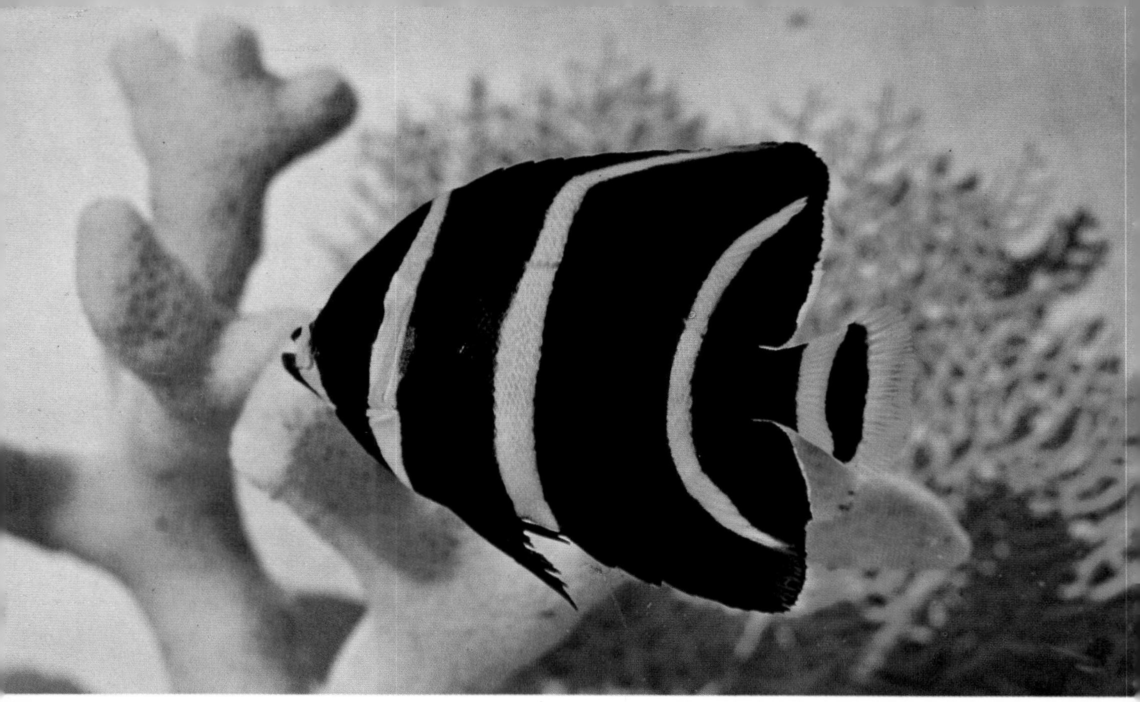

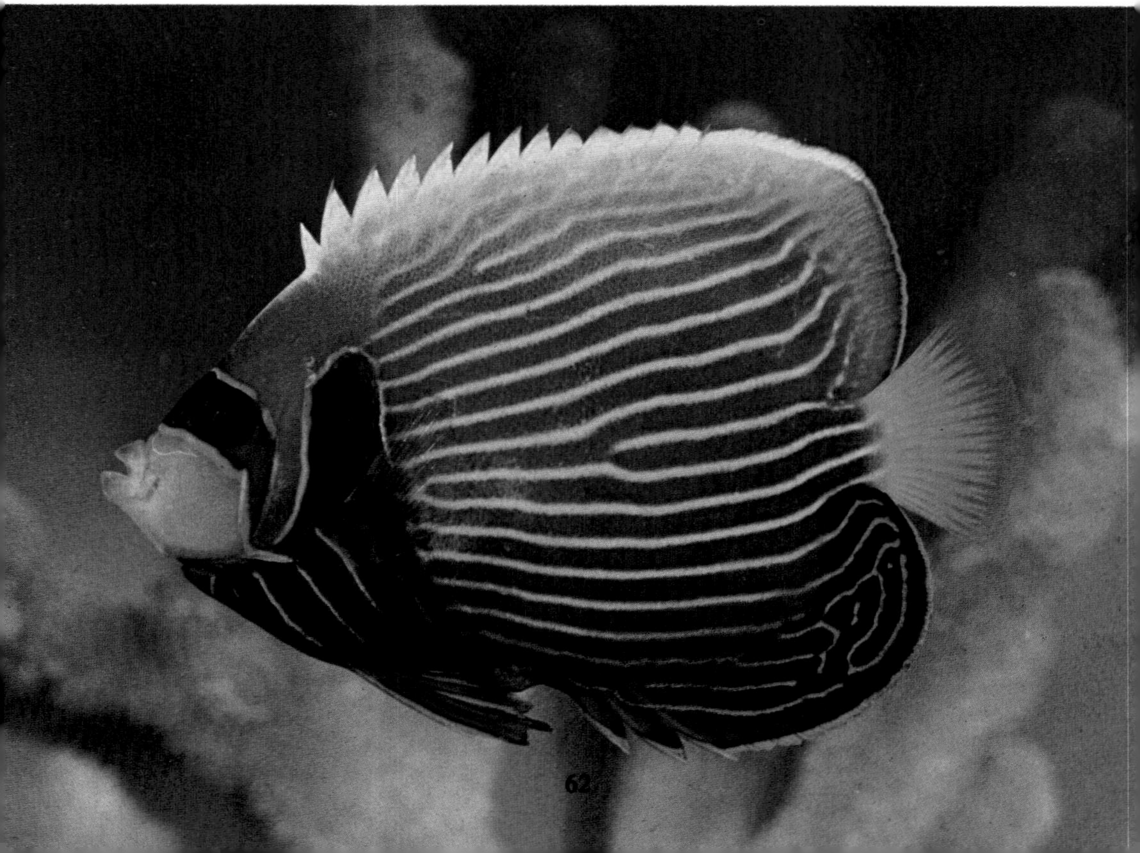

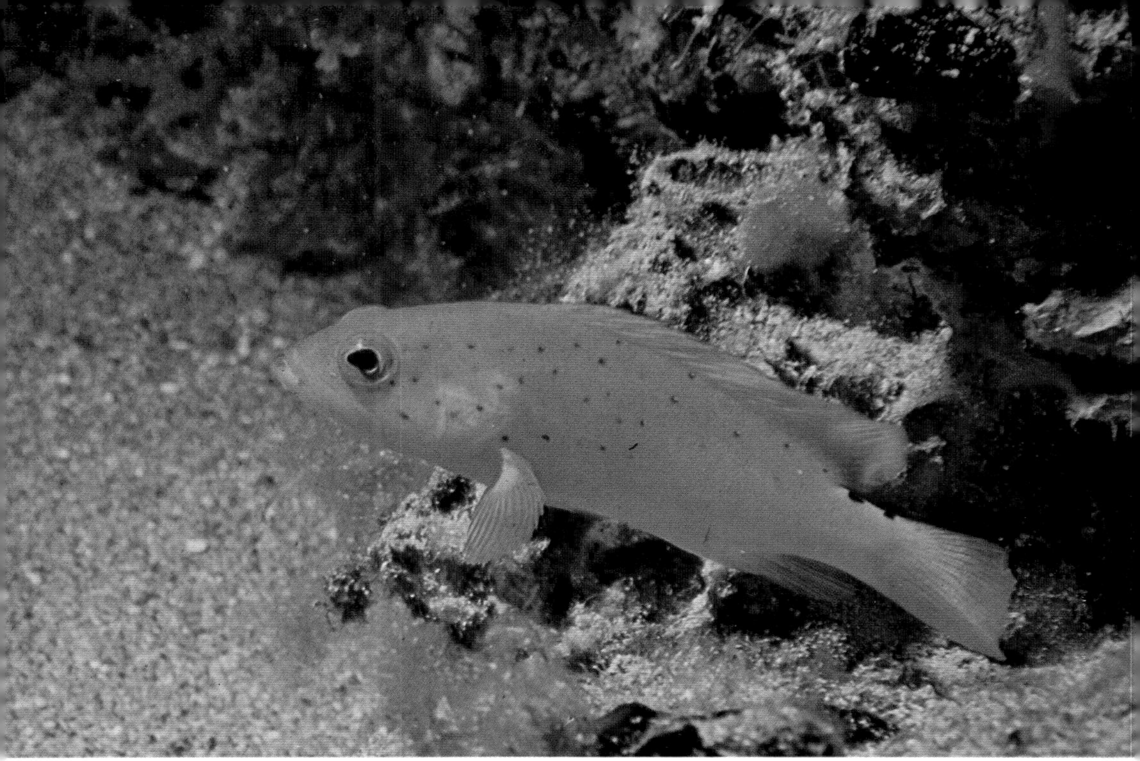

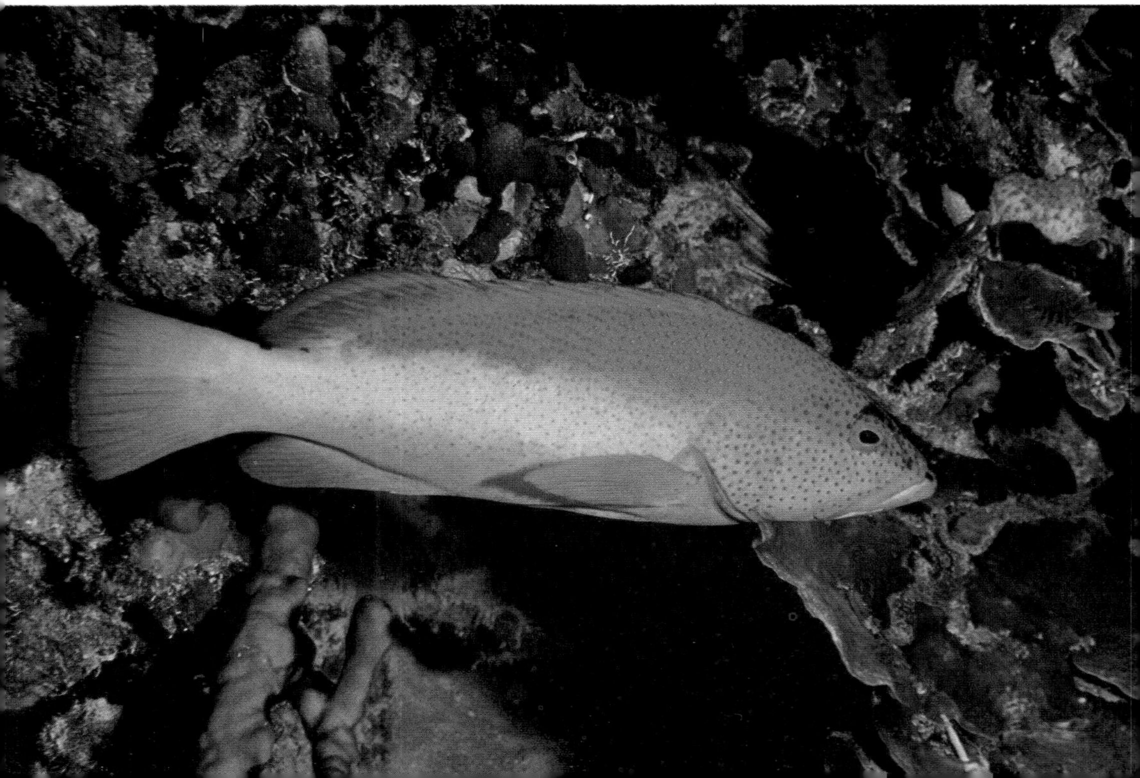

Pacific Marine Tropicals

exaggerated, for as Dr. Earl Herald pointed out, it misses the target more often than not. Moreover, individuals vary in their ability to hit the mark and in the number of shots they can get away within a certain period. The mechanism and anatomical structure that enable this fish to act like an animated fire hose were discovered by two U.S. ichthyologists, Drs. Hugh M. Smith and George S. Myers. Smith showed that water was forcibly ejected from the mouth when the gill covers were squeezed suddenly. Myers then found that when the tongue was pressed against a groove in the roof of the mouth a small tube was formed. A sudden compression of the gill covers forces water out through this channel, the drops sometimes carrying more than 15 feet!

Heidger and Heusser of the University of Zurich used high speed motion picture photography in order to determine the nature of the jet of water. Up until this time it was unknown whether it was a single stream, a single drop, or a series of drops. According to their findings, the fish spouts a single jet of water that breaks up within two to four inches into a spray and several large drops The large drops leave the spray behind and pass on to hit the target.

Archerfishes can be trained to eat a variety of foods, including hamburger, that has been thrown against the inside of their tank. Live insects or mealworms are preferred, however. After a fish has become accustomed to its surroundings, it will almost always shoot water at an insect held over the tank with tweezers. These fishes do best in brackish or salt water. Their natural habitat ranges from India to the northeastern tip of Australia. About a half dozen species are known.

The target perch *(Therapon jarbua)* is another extremely hardy fish and good aquarium specimen. The species eats well, grows in captivity, and is constantly on the move.

Target perch are silvery, with three dark longitudinal bands on the sides, each of which is curved slightly downwards in the center. These dark bands produce a target-like pattern when the fish is viewed from above. Found all the way from the Red Sea to Samoa, this species grows to about 10 inches.

Although most catfishes are found solely in fresh water, two families of them live in the sea. The one most well known to aquarists is the family Plotsidae, to which the little yellow-striped, stinging catfish, *Plotosus anguillaris,* belongs. In its dorsal and pectoral fins this fish has spines equipped with venom glands. A sting from one of these results in an extremely painful wound.

Plotosus anguillaris is an active swimmer, almost always on the move in a schooling formation. When frightened, members of a school take refuge in a hole or under a rock; if these are absent, they attempt to get under each other, which results in a tumbling, swirling mass of catfish.

A good aquarium fish, this catfish eats almost any food and grows large in

Invertebrates

captivity. The adult length is about 10 inches. It ranges from Fiji and Samoa to the Red Sea.

The hawkfishes resemble somewhat the scorpionfishes and have many features in common with them. Most are too large for home aquariums, but one, *Paracirrhites arcatus,* grows to only four inches and lives well in the confines of a tank. It is a sedentary species, usually found perched atop a rock or coral head, from whence it makes occasional short dashes for food. It prefers live fishes, but it can be induced to eat cut fish and shrimp.

Although the coloration of this fish is highly variable, it usually has a rosy or rusty red body color, with green fins and a green, white-bordered ovoid patch extending upwards and backwards from the eye.

Yellow-striped grunt.

Most beginning attempts to establish a marine aquarium include a number of invertebrate animals that are usually indiscriminately placed in the tank with the fish. The result in too many cases is fouling of the water, captured fish, and death to many or all of the inhabitants from some "unknown cause."

Carefully selected, many interesting invertebrates may be kept in a fish aquarium, but there are others that are best confined to a separate tank.

Small hermit crabs are readily available wherever there is ocean water and their value as scavengers makes them worth considering. Most of the tropicals will do their own scavenging, however, so that the addition of special fish or other animals for this purpose is not absolutely necessary. The hermit crab is interesting in its life struggle for a new shell to fit its growth, and will usually abandon the old one for a slightly larger, colorful tropical shell when placed in the tank. Old shells should be removed at once and a continual check made of the hermit so that if death occurs the dead one is removed without delay.

Many species of small, brightly colored shrimp are found in Maine waters, and one in particular, the larger red and white banded coral shrimp *(Stenopus hispidus),* will add harmless and colorful interest to the coral and sand where it will do a fine job of scavenging. The coral shrimp's habit of systematically molting its entire exoskeleton every month or so will at first make the aquarist start when he approaches the

Invertebrates

tank one morning to find two shrimps where there was but one the night before. The skin comes off in its entirety and will be found perched on the coral in a life-like attitude, complete with eyes, legs, feelers and all, while its ghostly counterpart is happily eating nearby and rapidly growing a replacement shell. A pair of banded coral shrimp kept by one of the authors shed their skeletons in the same night and created a matter for interesting speculation to imagine one helping the other out of its clothes.

The beauty of the sea flower, or anemone, is often sought to add its delicate tubular "petals" to the background of the jagged coral. It is the authors' contention, however, that even in an aerated tank the anemones produce a secretion that will affect the fish eventually over a period of several months, and they will also generate a slightly detectable anemone odor in the water in a much shorter time.

The suggestion here is to keep anemones in a separate invertebrate tank, where they usually thrive on bits of raw meat dropped on their tentacles a few times each week. In India one large specimen has been kept in this manner for more than 15 years. In addition, some of the treatments prescribed for fish diseases are deadly to invertebrates, especially the anemones. Therefore treatment is simplified if a special invertebrate tank can be maintained.

Among the most bizarre and interesting creatures of the sea are the octopuses, whose maintenance in captivity presents a real challenge to both the home aquarist and the public aquarist. One should not attempt to keep an octopus unless he has had considerable experience with marine fishes and some of the hardier invertebrates.

Octopuses are very delicate animals that are sensitive to nitrogenous and other waste products of fish. Therefore the first step in keeping them is to provide them with a tank of their own, the bigger the better. Also, they apparently are sensitive to their own products of metabolism as well as their sepia, which they discharge when disturbed. Therefore their tank should be given good aeration and the water circulated rapidly through a power filter. The filter bed should contain crushed shells or limestone chips to maintain the pH, fine sand and nylon wool to remove suspended matter, and activated carbon or charcoal to eliminate the dissolved wastes. If a fresh suppy of sea water is needed, one of the commercial salt water mixes can be used.

The main diet of the octopus is crabs. If they are alive so much the better, but they can be persuaded to take dead ones. They can also be induced to eat living or freshly killed goldfish.

In nature octopuses actively hunt crabs; when one is seen they jet to a position above it and settle like a parachute, with arms and web outstretched. They also lie in wait and whip out an arm to seize the crab with their suckers. Usually the octopus will bite through the shell of the crab with its horny beak and then proceed to disarticulate it, extracting the meat from the farthest reaches of the legs and shell with the tips of its arms. To make this easier, the octopus secretes an enzyme that helps to digest the tissue and loosen it from the shell.

The octopus has a poison gland that it uses for killing its prey. This poison apparently affects the nervous system. Crabs injected with it go limp at first, then have convulsions and die. It does not seem necessary for the octopus to bite for the poison to work. It can be exuded into the water while the crab is held, and the poison takes effect almost immediately.

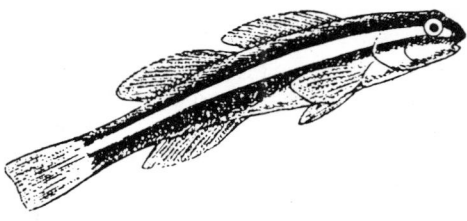

Neon goby, Gobiosoma oceanops.

An octopus during the day will usually assume the color of its background. It can change from sand color to brown or russet, or show a pattern of these. At night these creatures are quite often an opalescent blue-green. An octopus that is constantly changing color is a healthy one. An alarmed octopus or one that is near death turns a cadaverous gray.

The octopus can change his color quite rapidly. These color changes are caused by the contraction and expansion of the chromatophores, or pigment cells. In the octopus and other cephalopods, the walls of the pigment cell are controlled by muscle fibers. When these muscles are relaxed, the elasticity of the cell wall causes the pigment to be concentrated in a very small area so as to be almost invisible. When the muscles contract they expand the chromatophore, spreading the pigment over a larger area.

The rapidity of color changes—it takes less than a second for a chromatophore to expand—is due to direct neuromuscular control, with the primary stimulus being received by the eye or, to a lesser degree, the suckers.

Like a mouse, an octopus can squeeze through an unbelievably small hole or crack. It is therefore necessary to keep a tight cover on its tank and to weight or tie the cover down. The tip of an arm once started in a crack will continue to work and push and shove until the crack is widened far enough for the body to slip through.

A glass cover for the tank and plastic screen over the space left for the air lines is a necessity, for an octopus is capable of climbing out of the tank and half way up the living room wall.

Small sea slugs sometimes possess indescribably beautiful patterns, and if only the extremely tiny ones are kept they will not harm the fishes, who will ignore them. Larger specimens, including the free-swimming sea pigeons, will create a slime and are capable of ejecting ink much like the octopus. These are best confined to the invertebrate tank, where

Marine Plants

they will feed on algae.

Many forms of worms are collected with characteristics ranging from beauty to just plain wormy. Some of the former secrete about themselves an inflexible tube of sand or lime. These are known as plume worms, from the feathery mouth parts that protrude from the tube and that feed for the most part on plankton in the ocean and brine shrimp in the aquarium. Material should be afforded for making additions to the tube, either fine calcareous or siliceous sand, depending on the type of tube. If placed in a glass tube, many worms will make themselves at home and carry on all the bodily processes in plain view with breathing, pumping, and stomach rumblings putting on quite a show.

Snails are not recommended, for they tend to die from lack of food in a clean fish aquarium, but in the invertebrate tank they will live successfully on algae that should be afforded them.

Certain shellfish, notably the oyster, will act as rather efficient filters in the invertebrate tank but must be immediately removed if death occurs, or they can be opened up if sufficient scavengers are present.

A beautiful little scarlet-fringed swimming scallop known as *Lima scabra* will add a brilliancy and an unusual form to the invertebrate tank but will require, along with the oysters, that a well-crushed shellfish be added to the tank occasionally to supply the fine edible material that is filtered out and digested as food.

The actual necessity of plants, save for psychological reasons or in rare cases as food, in either the fresh- or saltwater aquariums, is doubtful, as shown by Dr. James W. Atz.

Although plant life does help remove nitrogenous waste material excreted by the fishes, most of the ammoniates in solution and carbon dioxide are readily passed off as gases through the application of artificial aeration.

The coral fishes for the most part are ignorant of plant life in their natural environment, save for tiny algae, and are burdened by the attempts of the aquarist to introduce foliage into a marine aquarium.

There are instances, however (a community of grass fishes such as sea horses or trunkfishes for example), where the environment is more natural when it includes growing plants. This being the case, it is well to discuss the possibilities of raising marine grasses and also some of the larger leafy algae.

The flowering plant *Thalassia testudinum,* commonly called blade or turtle grass, is plentiful along the shores of southern Florida, but it cannot be successfully transplanted as it is found to the aquarium, where it dies and rapidly pollutes the water. It is, fortunately, a seed-bearing plant, and at certain seasons of the year green pods from this plant about one inch in diameter may be found rolling about on the sandy bottom surrounding the grass beds. Opening one of these pods will reveal a number of brown seeds about the size of large peas,

Marine Plants

and these, if placed in a container of ocean water, will sprout a small shoot and soon display the bright green blades of the grass. As growth continues the larger of the three blades that emerge will turn brown and die, and a new one will appear at the base of the seed. This cycle continues for the life of the plant and requires picking off the dead leaf at the base and removing it from the water to prevent decay and pollution.

If the sprouted seed is planted in sand, and if after several months the soil about the plant is examined, it will be found to be discolored with a black, foul-smelling stain. This is caused by hydrogen sulphide gas that is probably generated by the decay of the seed skin in the absence of sufficient oxygen. If the seed has protruded slightly above the sand during this growth a white fungus may be observed surrounding the area. This fungus apparently thrives in the presence of hydrogen sulphide gas but in itself does not directly hurt the fishes, for they often pick at it and will clean up an area where it has developed. It is, however, an indication that undesirable gases are present and that decay and pollution are occurring.

If after sprouting leaves the seeds are rinsed and replanted in clean sand, new ocean water added, and the seed part covered with at least one-half inch of sand, the gas will usually be prevented from reaching the surface and supporting the white fungus, and the water will be able to support fish life safely.

White fluorescent light increases the rate of growth of this plant while apparently not encouraging unwanted algae formation. A blue angelfish some two inches long was kept in perfect health in this manner in a two-gallon unaerated glass bowl with six individual plants. The container was cleaned once each month, however; the sand was rinsed and cleaned, the plants replanted, and the used water completely replaced with fresh water.

There are a number of leafy, nonvascular green algae, all in the genus *Caulerpa,* that do well in aquaria if left undisturbed. These are characterized by leafy projections that emerge from a main runner that is supplied with holdfasts. These plants take on many attractive forms and can be collected in shallow water grass flats where only the growing tip of the runner, along with a number of leaves and holdfasts, should be taken.

Planted in sand, the plant usually grows only at one end of the runner, with new leaves and holdfasts emerging at spaced intervals. The opposite end of the plant will eventually die at a rate equal to the growth of the other end, and the dead part should be pinched off at regular intervals to prevent decay in the water.

Most of the coral or grass fishes will pick at and eat these leafy algae while ignoring the grass, so that only the tiny tropicals or larger fishes, such as the sea horses and others that will not damage them, should be placed with the algae.

In addition to the caulerpas, there are several other algae that are attractive and

Disease Control

will live for varying periods of time if given enough light. One of these is *Udotea,* a fan-like plant that is attached to the bottom by a short stalk. Another is the shaving brush, *Penicillus.* These plants should be collected from the deepest water possible or from a shaded area such as under a bridge or pier. These specimens will be accustomed to reduced light and will hold up better under aquarium conditions. A special fluorescent plant bulb will do much toward providing the proper light.

Should the fishes be placed with the algae the water must be aerated, for some of these plants seem to generate waste gases during the night that may eventually cause the fishes to suffocate.

Caulerpa, *a marine plant.*

While some deaths in the marine aquarium are attributable to internal or external diseases, many others are due to poor housekeeping and accidental deaths. Some fishes die from suffocation as a result of a crowded tank or overfeeding. Poisoning from tobacco, insect sprays, or a newly painted room is the cause of many fatalities. We have seen a fish go into shock and die from careless handling or sometimes from the shock occasioned when the light over its tank is suddenly turned on. Most of these things are more or less under the control of the hobbyist, and deaths due to them can be prevented by using a little common sense.

There are available on the market several preparations for the control and cure of diseases of marine tropicals. These are put up in convenient units with specific directions for use. Your local dealer should be able to advise you as to which one to use.

Fishes are afflicted, as are most other animals, by internal tumors, degeneration of certain organs, and insidious diseases, that are not recognized until the fish is dead, or almost dead. There is very little the hobbyist can do about these conditions, and it is best to develop a philosophical attitude about them rather than spend a lot of time and money on cure-alls.

There are a few conditions, however, that can definitely be recognized, treated, and cured.

Parasites

Probably the most common of

Disease Control

parasitic diseases and one that will reach epidemic proportions in a very short time is the one caused by a dinoflagellate of the genus *Oodinium,* a protozoan of the order Dinoflagellida (from the Greek *dinos*—whirling, and Latin *flagellum*—a whip). The dinoflagellates differ from other flagellates in having their flagella housed in transverse grooves. They usually move through the water with a whirling, tumbling motion.

Oodinium attaches itself to a fish and soon discards the flagella. It then becomes more firmly attached and receives nourishment from the fish by root-like processes. After reaching a size of .1 mm it becomes detached and divides repeatedly, forming more than 250 young. It is at this free-swimming stage that it is susceptible to treatment.

Fishes infected with *Oodinium* have a characteristic behavior. They appear to be in distress. They huddle together or hide under a rock. Their respiration is labored, because the organisms attach to the gills, and they make short fast dashes, scraping their sides along the walls and bottom of the tank. In severe infections the entire body will be covered with the parasites, and the fishes will appear almost white.

The best and cheapest treatment for this disease is copper, used in the form of copper sulfate or some other copper salt. The amount of copper sulfate to be used can be calculated by the formula:

$$X = \frac{V \times P \times 3.93}{1000}$$

Where X = weight of copper sulfate in grams
V = volume of tank in liters
P = parts per million (ppm) of copper desired
3.93 = number of grams of copper sulfate containing one gram of copper.

The volume of your tank in liters can be found by multiplying its gallon capacity by 3.785. A dosage of .15 ppm is ideal for most fishes.

For small tanks the proper amount of copper can be added by making a stock solution and adding a certain amount of this to your tank. To achieve a concentration of .15 ppm, dissolve one gram of copper sulfate (a druggist can weigh it out for you) in a pint (16 ozs.) of water. Of this stock solution, use one cc. (20 drops) for each gallon of salt water. Remember to consider rocks, coral, shells, and sand when figuring the volume of the tank. It is best to remove these decorations when treating with copper, as they will combine with the copper to form insoluble carbonates. This will decrease the strength and effectiveness of your solution and give the water a slightly milky appearance. If it is not practical to remove the decorations, add a quarter gram of citric acid crystals to the stock solution. This will reduce the precipitation of copper. If you do not wish to make your own solution, commercially packaged ones are available.

It takes about seven days for *Oodinium* to develop into the free-swimming stage;

Disease Control

copper treatment should be maintained at least this long, and a 10-day treatment is recommended. Actually it is not necessary to change the water or otherwise remove the copper unless invertebrates are to be introduced into the tank. As noted above, any coral in the tank will gradually remove the copper. Small quantities of copper are often fatal to invertebrates.

Saltwater fishes also are attacked by a fluke known as *Benedenia (Epibdella) millini*. This is a monogenetic trematode, that is, it is a fluke that has a relatively simple life cycle and a single host. Members of this group are chiefly external parasites of turtles, fishes, and amphibians.

Benedenia attacks the eyes and body of most marine fishes, although many are immune. It attaches by two anterior suckers, which are unarmed, and one posterior sucker, which bears three pairs of large spines and 14 small hooks. The adults are 5 mm ($\frac{1}{5}$ inch) long and although almost transparent they can be seen, especially on the eyes of the fishes.

Fishes infected with *Benedenia* show the same behavior as those with *Oodinium*. In addition the eyes are more severely affected and become filmed over and inflamed; they finally bulge and burst. An old treatment was to bathe the affected fish either in fresh water or very strong salt water. However, this fluke can be easily controlled by the same copper treatment as has been described for *Oodinium*. The entire life cycle lasts 10 to 12 days.

Occasionally sea horses will be seen with *Argulus* crawling on them. This is a brown crustacean, half the size of the end of a pencil, that is extremly difficult to eradicate. Any treatment strong enough to kill *Argulus* will usually injure the host. The parasites swim from host to host and leave their eggs deposited on the sides of the tanks or on rocks. These eggs appear as two parallel lines, not necessarily straight, of short brown dashes. About the only way to eliminate *Argulus* is to remove the sea horses and pick off the parasites with a tweezers. The tank should be drained and thoroughly scrubbed to get rid of any eggs.

Other Ailments

Raw lesions on the fins or body caused by bacterial infection should be treated by swabbing the infected area with aqueous mercurochrome, Merthiolate, or potassium permanganate. Treatment in the tank with Aureomycin, Terramycin, and sulfa compounds may be more practical where several fishes are involved. Limited success has been reported using acriflavin as a fungicide following the manufacturer's prescribed dosage.

Popeye is apparely due to two things. One is hemorrhage produced by gas in the capillaries in the eye socket. Sometimes a strong circulating pump will supersaturate the water with air, which is then taken up by the fishes. At the reduced pressure inside the fish, the air is released as fine bubbles, which can cause blockage and rupture of the capillaries. Pumps should be checked for leaks on the intake side. The other cause is bacterial infection, and in this case the eye should be treated with sulfathiazole, ½ teaspoon to a gallon, or the eye painted with five per cent argyrol solution.

Injuries sustained in battles between the fishes or while they are being captured will usually heal rapidly in a healthy aquarium without treatment. The fins particularly have an amazing ability to regenerate. An apparently missing tail, for example, will often attain its original size within a couple of weeks. This seemingly fantastic ability to speedily repair a badly damaged organ or, in the lower animals, to completely regenerate a lost part, can often be observed in the aquarium. The replacement of the entire leg of a shrimp or crayfish, the growth of a whole starfish from one broken arm (provided that the arm contains part of the central disc), generation of a new digestive system which had been discharged by a sea cucumber, and many more examples stand in testimony to the tenacity of life marine organisms display living in the most competitive environment in the world—the sea.

One eye of a large wrasse was injured on the coral during a transfer to another tank used for photographing the fish. The next morning the damaged eye was swollen and protruding from the eye socket. The entire surface was a slate

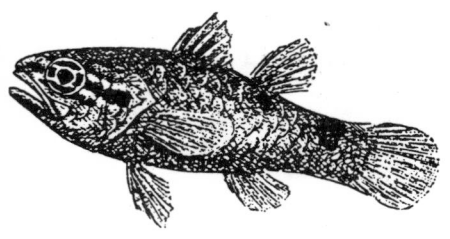

Spotted cardinal fish, Apogon maculatus.

gray and complete opaque. It was assumed that the eye was lost, but the following morning at feeding time the wrasse was up for food using a perfect pair of eyes.

74

Underwater Conservation

Anyone who makes a serious attempt at collecting marine life by diving or wading with a water glass in shallow water is struck by the seemingly inexhaustible supply of fish life that swarms before his eyes. In an effort to secure the wanted specimens, rocks are overturned, sponges are torn up, and coral heads uprooted, creating what the individual might consider only temporary havoc to the immediate area. Strangely enough, thoughtless actions such as these have laid waste for years to come areas that in times past were lush collecting grounds.

Wherever an area is found to be particularly prolific of small tropicals, whether an outer reef eight miles from the shore or a patch of sponges but a few hundred yards out, it can be assumed that this is a spawning bed for coral fishes. It is this, primarily, because suitable cover is afforded for protection and food is plentiful for the young fishes. Turning over a rock and leaving it thus, for instance, will kill much of the algae and minute animals on which the small fishes feed. Tearing up sponges and corals, of course, kills them and additional cover and food are lost to the area.

Moreover, the adult fishes will most likely refuse to spawn in an area that has been molested extensively, driven much by the same instinct that all wild animals display where breeding grounds are violated.

It is a singularly weird feeling to return to an area that had been a thriving underwater community but a few weeks before and find only a few lonely scavengers picking hungrily at the torn stumps of what had been protecting canopies of finger sponge. The same sensation can be experienced while exploring the deserted mines and cabins in the hills near Virginia City in Nevada—here is a ghost town underwater!

The hope is that the public realizes the need for practicing conservation, even underwater.

Suggestions while collecting are to right any rock overturned and to use finesse in dislodging the fishes from the corals and sponges particularly, rather than merely tearing up the homes of many to secure one individual.

Practicing these simple considerations will maintain your favorite collecting grounds as a constant source for obtaining young specimens and guarantee that a teeming underwater world will await your every visit with fascinating reward.

Intelligence in Fishes

A surprising capacity for learning is displayed by most marine fishes; among these, the angelfishes are most conspicuous.

The routine of feeding the fishes daily offers an opportunity to watch the learning process and to observe the keen attention that they give to all that goes on in and about the tank.

Fishes that are new to the society, after acquaintance has been made with other members, first learn that there is such a thing as a water surface through which they cannot swim, a fact most of them would have remained ignorant of, living out their lives in deep grottoes of the coral reef.

Eating the unfamiliar flake food is, at first, awkward and unnatural, and there is hesitation in poking their noses into the strange air-water division between their world and ours. Soon, however, many are projecting their dorsal fins high out of the water and are confidently pecking at the food.

An association between food and the person who feeds them is rapidly made and will often reach the extent of their distinguishing that person from others who visit the tank less regularly.

Training the fishes to take food from your clean fingers is easily accomplished and, as a matter of further interest, so is coaching them to permit you to scratch their backs. A large blue angelfish known by one of the authors delighted in having his back scratched and would slowly back up tail first to a finger when it was dipped into the water and would roll over on his side to make sure all surfaces were duly covered. This action, by the way, is the same exhibited to one of the parasite pickers.

The extent to which certain species of marine fishes may be tamed was published some time ago in a popular weekly magazine. It presented the story of a man in Australia who for years has been wading out on the sea shore near his home to feed some large fish that would return year after year. Some of these had become so tame that they swam into his arms and lay still when he lifted them from the water to be photographed, as the pictures in the article proved.

Among saltwater fishes, groupers become especially tame. Many learn to recognize divers who frequent an area and allow themselves to be petted. French scientist-diver Jacques Cousteau and his team of divers once made a pet of a grouper, which they called Ulysses, but it became so much of a pest that they had to cage it while they were working underwater.

Further Reading

Your tropical fish shop will have many other books about marine fishes and aquaria. T.F.H. publishes the following recommended books.

THE ENCYCLOPEDIA OF MARINE INVERTEBRATES
By a panel of experts, each specializing in individual phyla
ISBN 0-87666-707-X
TFH H-951

This excellent and enormously colorful book ranges widely over the invertebrate field and provides detailed information on the natural history and taxonomy of every invertebrate group of interest to marine aquarists, professional biologists, naturalists, skin divers and collectors and those involved in the marine aquarium hobby on a commercial level. A superb compilation of vital information and beautiful photos, this book is also an excellent identification guide.
Hard cover, 5½ x 8", 736 pages
Over 600 full-color photos, many line drawings.

SALT WATER AQUARIUM FISHES
By Drs. Herbert R. Axelrod and Warren E. Burgess
ISBN 0-87666-138-X
TFH H-914

Contents: Why A Salt-Water Aquarium? Setting Up Your Marine Aquarium Water—The Main Ingredient. Some Principles And Practices Of Aquarium Management For Marine Aquariums. Feeding Salt-Water Fishes. Diseases Of Salt-Water Aquarium Fishes. Fishes For The Marine Aquarium.

A very complete book, for the medium-level aquarist who has one or two salt-water tanks and wants to know the best fishes to keep and the best techniques for keeping them. This book has gone through many editions, and each edition brings many changes. Modern and up-to-date, and very popular with beginning and medium-level marine aquarists. Written on a high school level.
Hard cover, 5½ x 8½", 440 pages
53 black and white photos
264 color photos

PACIFIC MARINE FISHES
By Dr. Warren E. Burgess and Dr. Herbert R. Axelrod

NOTE: The PACIFIC MARINE FISHES series is a planned group of 12 books (7 have already been published) covering the fishes of the Pacific Ocean. Following are the contents of Book 1 only— coverage by family of course varies from book to book in the series.
Family Dasyatidae (Stingrays). Family Orectolobidae (Wobbegongs And Catsharks). Family Congridae (Conger Eels). Family Muraenidae (Moray Eels). Family Moringuidae (Spaghetti Or Thrush Eels). Family Anomalopidae (Lantern-Eyes). Family Atherinidae (Silversides Or Hardyheads). Family Syngathidae (Pipefishes And Seahorses). Family Apogonidae (Cardinalfishes). Family Mulidae (Goatfishes). Family Nemipteridae (Butterfly-Bream). Family Pomadasyidae (Grunts, Sweetlips, Etc.). Family Chaetodontidae (Butterflyfishes). Family Pomacentridae (Anemonefishes And

Further Reading

Damselfishes). Family Blenniidae (Blennies). Family Acanthuridae (Surgeonfishes).
Hard cover, 8½ x 11"

THE MARINE AQUARIUM IN THEORY AND PRACTICE
By Dr. Cliff W. Emmens
ISBN 0-87666-446-X
TFH PS-735

Contents: THE TANK AND EQUIPMENT. THE WATER. WORKABLE MARINE SYSTEMS. HANDLING FISHES AND INVERTEBRATES. DISEASES AND PARASITES.

An unusually successful and popular book, written for the owner of a single or multiple marine aquarium setup. For the first time, the water chemistry, water physics, and theory of a miniature ocean is discussed by Prof. Emmens, who is chairman of the Veterinary Physiology Department of the University of Sydney in Australia. The book takes the reader through the marine aquarium problems step-by-step. Written on a high school level.
Hard cover, 8½ x 11", 208 pages
99 black and white photos,
191 color photos

EXOTIC MARINE FISHES
By Dr. Herbert R. Axelrod, Dr. Warren E. Burgess and Dr. Cliff W. Emmens
ISBN 0-87666-102-9
TFH H-938L (Looseleaf)
ISBN 0-87666-103-7
TFH H-938 (Hardbound, non-looseleaf)

Contents: STARTING A TROPICAL MARINE TANK—Collection And Use Of Salt Water. Artificial Sea Water. Treatment Of The Tank And Decorations. Tank Size And Shape. Lighting. Heating. Other Equipment. Aeration And Filtration. Sterilization. Sub-Sand Filters. Landscaping Of Tanks. THE TANK IN ACTION— Tank Sterility. Periodic Checks. New Arrivals. Removing Fishes. Fish Capacity Of Tanks. General Maintenance. The Biological Filter. Maintenance Of Sub-Sand Filters. Maintenance With Other Filters. Feeding The Fishes. Diseases And Parasites. White Spot Disease. Velvet Disease. Non-Specific Itches. Bacterial Infections. Lymphocystis. *Ichthyophonus.* Exophthalmos (Pop-Eye). *Saprolegnia* Or Fungus. Argulus. Shock. Poisoning In Tanks. TANK INHABITANTS—Invertebrates. Anemones. Living Coral. Worms. Sea Squirts And Sponges. Mollusks. Crustaceans. Echinoderms. Fishes. Families Of Fishes. Purchasing Fishes. ALPHABETICAL CATALOGUE OF FISHES.

This book, available in both looseleaf and non-looseleaf form, is the most comprehensive and colorful book available about the marine aquarium hobby.
Hardcover and looseleaf, 5½ x 8½", 608 pages, 88 black and white photos, 477 color photos.

MARINE INVERTEBRATES
By U. Erich Friese
ISBN 0-87666-105-3
TFH PS-658

Contents: What Is An "Invertebrate"? Marine Invertebrates And The Aquarium. The Chemistry Of The Sea Water. Some Aquarium Technology. Phylum Protozoa. Metazoa And The Phylum Mesozoa.

Further Reading

Phylum Porifera. Phylum Cnidaria. Phylum Platyhelminthes. Phylum Nemertea. Phylum Nemathelminthes. Phylum Endoprocta. Phylum Annelida. Phylum Arthropoda. Phylum Mollusca. Phylum Phoronida. Phylum Echinodermata. Phylum Chordata.

This book is intended to give answers to aquarium hobbyists of all levels of experience concerning actual requirements of marine invertebrate animals from an aquarium management point of view plus an overall biological understanding of marine invertebrates. Ages 15 and up.
Soft cover, 8 x 5½", 240 pages
1 black and white photo,
119 color photos.

MARINE AQUARIUM GUIDE
By Frank de Graaf
ISBN 0-87666-805-8
TFH PL-2017

Contents: THEORY AND PRACTICE. Sea Water in Nature. Sea Water in the Aquarium. Preparing the Marine Aquarium. Setting up the Aquarium. Care of the Aquarium. AQUARIUM INHABITANTS. Populating the Tank. Fish Catalog. Aquarium Invertebrates.

Written with the nonprofessional in mind, this book makes the theory and practice of effectively controlling a tropical saltwater aquarium easy to understand. Both beginning and advanced hobbyists will benefit from the detailed discussions provided by the author, the curator of the Artis Aquarium. The reader will also find quick answers to many questions in the summaries provided at the end of several of the longer chapters.
Hard cover; 5½ x 8", 282 pages
54 color photos; 14 black and white photos;
28 line drawings.

BUTTERFLYFISHES OF THE WORLD
By Dr. Warren E. Burgess
ISBN 0-87666-470-2
TFH H-988

Contents: Introduction; Methods And Materials; Historical Review; Associated Families; Ecology And Behavior; Color And Pattern; Larvae; Anatomical Features Used In The Systematic Section; Systematic Section, Hybrids And Anomalies; List Of Taxa; Familial Relationships; Patterns Of Distribution Of The Family Chaetodontidae; Acknowledgements; Bibliography; Index.

This beautiful big book contains descriptions and photographs of every one of the 114 known species of butterflyfish in the world, making identification easy and certain. In addition, descriptions of every species, descriptions of behavior (pairing and aggression) are included with such vital data as feeding and tolerances and habitats. Years of research went into the making of this book, which is as valuable to aquarists as to ichthyologists. It has been referred to as a classic in its field and will be the standard work on the family Chaetodontidae for years to come.
Hard cover; 5½ x 8½", 832 pages
Illustrated with hundreds of color photos.

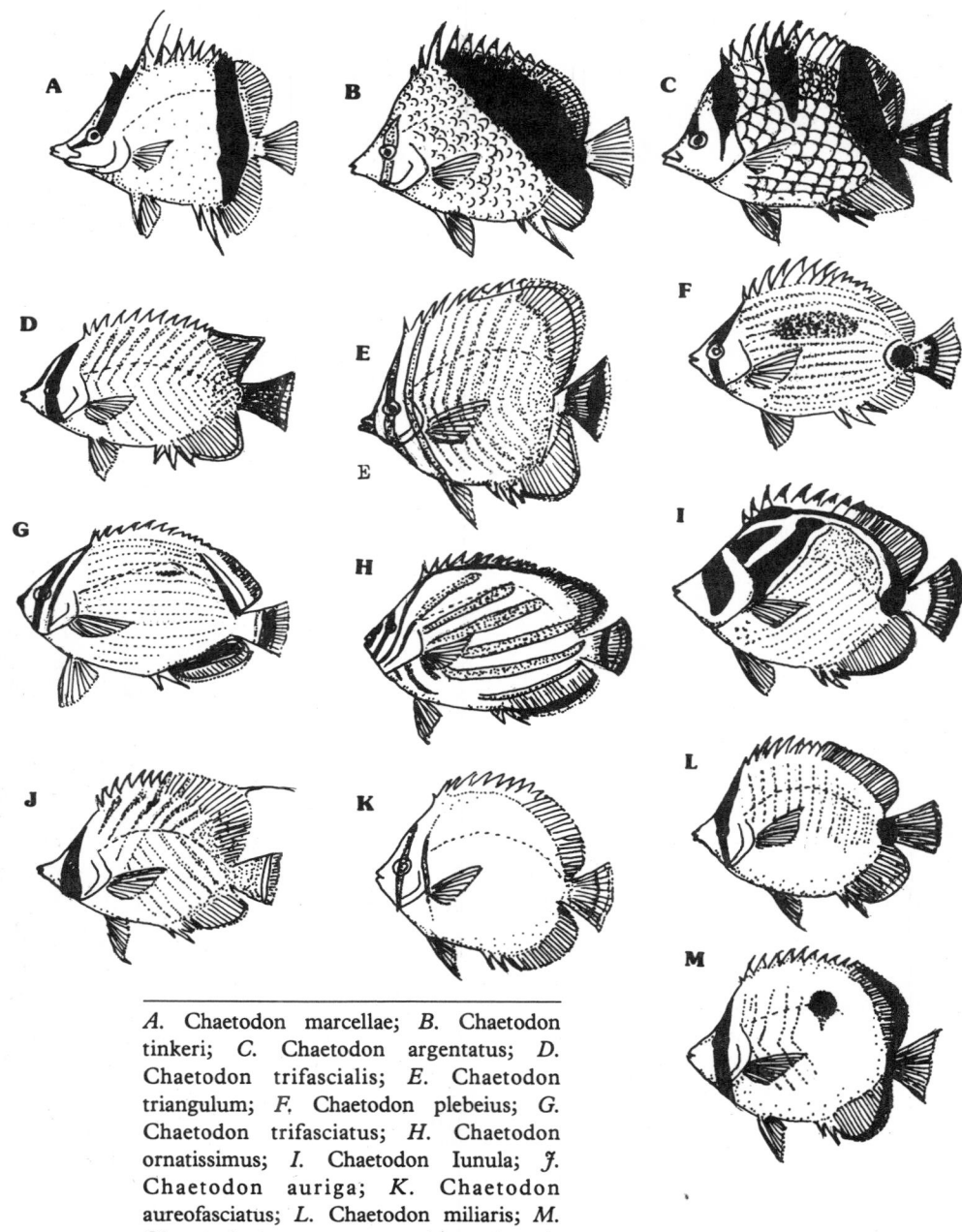

A. Chaetodon marcellae; B. Chaetodon tinkeri; C. Chaetodon argentatus; D. Chaetodon trifascialis; E. Chaetodon triangulum; F. Chaetodon plebeius; G. Chaetodon trifasciatus; H. Chaetodon ornatissimus; I. Chaetodon Iunula; J. Chaetodon auriga; K. Chaetodon aureofasciatus; L. Chaetodon miliaris; M. Chaetodon unimaculatus.

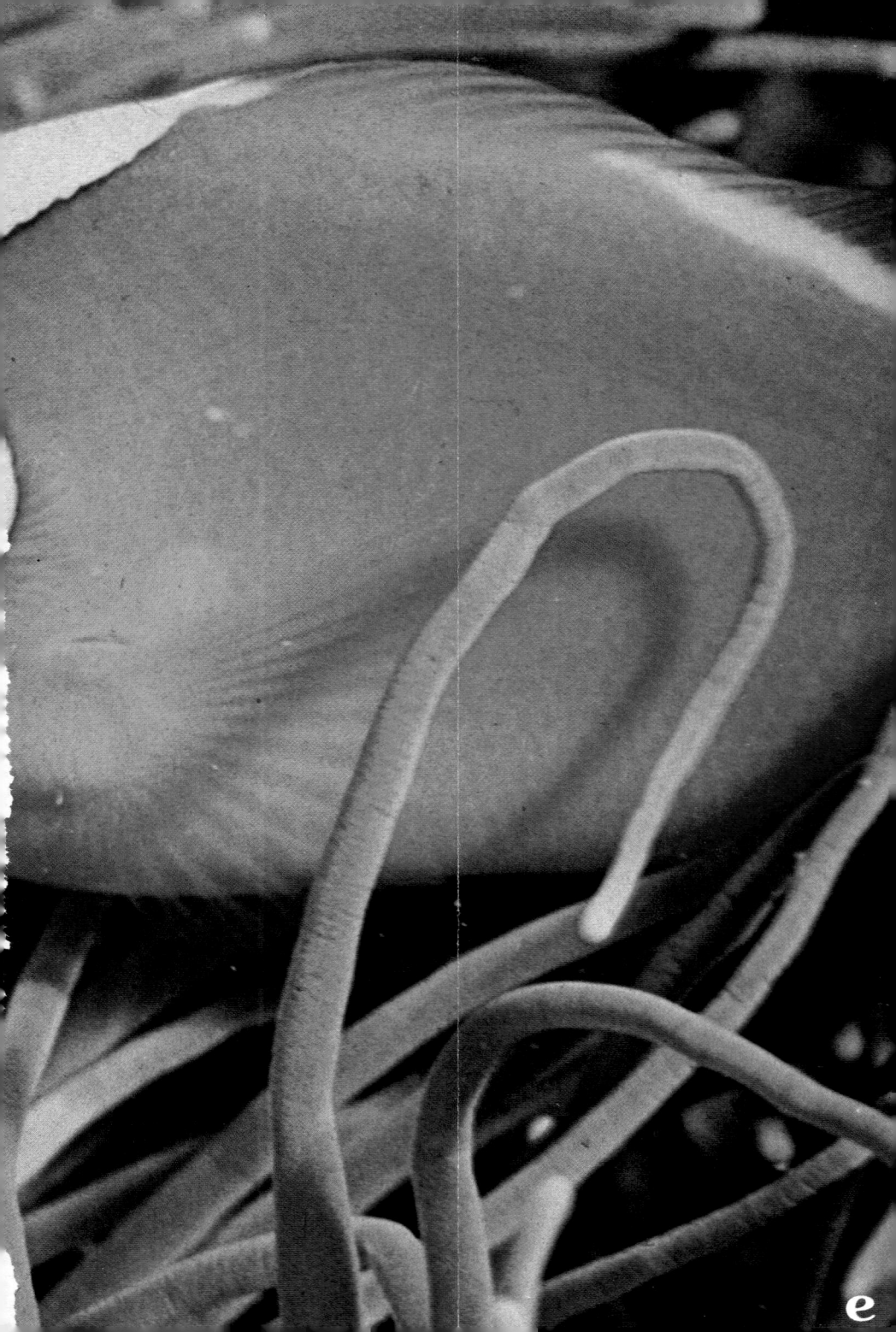

e